PRAISE FOn

DIVORCE: THINK FINANCIALLY, NOT EMOTIONALLY®

Divorce: Think Financially, Not Emotionally® is a wonderful guide for women seeking to secure their financial future. The book spans socioeconomic groups and delivers a message which is helpful to anyone making important life decisions in a rational and intelligent manner.

—Laura A. Wasser, Divorce Attorney to the Stars, including Maria Shriver, Heidi Klum, Angelina Jolie, Christina Aguilera, Britney Spears, and many others

I wish I had this book when I was going through my divorce. It would have made the learning curve much less steep! Knowing Jeffrey's expertise, any woman, whether going through a divorce or not, can benefit from this book!

—Sonja Morgan, star of Real Housewives of New York

Over the years, I have helped former New York City's Mayor Mike Bloomberg build several shelters for battered and abused women and their children, so I've seen firsthand the challenges these women face. This book is packed with practical advice for any woman who wants to better protect her assets during divorce, but it may be particularly valuable for women in abusive relationships, who typically find it more difficult to escape their situations and secure a sound financial future. What's more, Jeff Landers is donating a portion of the profits from this book to organizations helping women in abusive situations. I wholeheartedly applaud his efforts.

—*Liz Smith, Syndicated Columnist*

DIVORCE

THINK FINANCIALLY, NOT EMOTIONALLY®

Volume II

What women need to know about securing their financial future before, during, and after divorce

Jeffrey A. Landers, CDFA™

Sourced Media Books, LLC

ISBN 978-1-937458-92-8

LCCN 2012947648

Visit www.sourcedmediabooks.com

DEDICATION

This book is dedicated to all the women I have known who have struggled to break free from difficult and often abusive marriages. Your courage and determination have inspired me not only to complete this endeavor, but also to support various charities that help victims of domestic abuse.

SUPPORT FOR ABUSED WOMEN

A portion of the purchase price of each book sold is donated to various charities that help female victims of domestic abuse and their children.

CONTENTS

INTRODUCTION

Ever since *Divorce: Think Financially, Not Emotionally®—What Women Need To Know About Securing Their Financial Future Before, During, And After Divorce, Volume I*[1] was first published in 2012, I've heard from scores of women who are using it to successfully navigate the choppy waters of divorce. It has become an invaluable resource for women who want to better understand the financial implications of divorce so they can establish solid financial footing, both now and far into the future.

When I wrote *Divorce: Think Financially, Not Emotionally® Volume I*, I envisioned myself having a conversation with a client. I wanted the book to have a personal appeal, as though I was sitting across the table, sharing my expertise directly with you, the reader . . .

And now, I want that conversation to continue.

In *Divorce: Think Financially, Not Emotionally® Vol-*

ume II, I add more insight into the most important issues covered in *Volume I*, and I discuss many completely new topics, as well. Throughout the following chapters, you'll find essential information that every divorcing woman needs to know, including:

» Why you might want to keep a secret fund
» What you can and cannot withdraw from joint accounts
» The financial impacts of moving out of the marital home
» The pros and cons of filing first
» How to divide stock, stock options and restricted stock
» Student loans: Are they part of marital debt?
» Ways to protect inheritances and gifts
» How being a stay-at-home mom can affect your divorce and your financial future
» Special considerations for women who earn more than their husbands
» How dual citizenship impacts divorce
» . . . And much more!

I understand that thinking financially is not always easy, particularly if you're in the early stages of divorce, when you're probably experiencing anger, betrayal, loss, shock, numbness, confusion, panic— or a combination of them all. But even if thinking financially is not always easy, it *is* possible . . . and this book will show you how. You'll learn that with a little guidance, the proper planning and a sound strategy, you'll be able to emerge from your divorce in the best financial shape possible. Turn the page and start looking forward to that bright future today.

Note: This book is for informational purposes only and does not constitute legal advice. If you require legal advice, retain a lawyer licensed in your jurisdiction. The opinions expressed are solely those of the author, who is not an attorney.

A portion of the purchase price of each book sold will be donated to various charities that help female victims of domestic abuse and their children.

Visit http://ThinkFinancially.com to see all my divorce-related books, including any new releases, and for information about online eLearning courses, live events and other resources to help you Think Financially, Not Emotionally® before, during, and after your divorce.

PREPARING
FOR DIVORCE

*Volume I covers the essentials of preparing for divorce,
including the financial steps you need to take to get
organized, the four key players for your divorce team, and
how to protect your credit. In Volume II, let's dig a little
deeper and explore the financial impacts of divorce versus
separation and long-term separation, the advantages—
and disadvantages!—of filing first, other experts who can
contribute to your divorce team . . . and more.*

CHAPTER 1

BEWARE OF LONG-TERM SEPARATION LIMBO AND WHY YOU MUST PICK ONE: LEGAL SEPARATION OR DIVORCE

We all know married couples who aren't exactly "together" any more—even though they're not exactly divorced, either. These couples seem to have found a way to live separate lives within their legal marriage, each getting some of what they want out of life apart, and yet still showing up together at significant events as needed or keeping up appearances "for the kids."

We all also know that "breaking up is hard to do," as the old song goes. Divorce is not only emotionally tumultuous, but, frankly, it's a heck of a lot of work, as well. There's a tremendous amount to do, legally, financially, logistically, and otherwise. The stress and upheaval may be so daunting that there would seem to be no downside to avoiding it, if you can. In fact, some people seem to sidestep divorce completely by staying separated—and not just for a few months to a year, but for year, after year, after year! Is this a good idea? Are they onto something?

Well, as a Divorce Financial Strategist™[1], I can tell you that there are numerous downsides to "separation limbo," which is the term I use to describe what happens when spouses remain legally married, but live apart from one another without the benefit of a legal separation agreement. As I've seen time and time again, when there's no formal legal agreement that defines the terms of the separation, postponing divorce indefinitely can lead to financial disaster. Why? Because:

During a long separation without a legal separation agreement, you have no control over what your husband does with marital assets, including how he might hide them.

As long as you remain apart without a legal separation agreement, you'll have no idea what your husband is earning, spending, selling, buying, or investing—unless he chooses to tell you. You could be totally in the dark . . . and totally in trouble, especially if you live in a Community Property State and are liable for his debts.

Also, while it is underhanded, deplorable, and illegal, it is not at all unusual for husbands to go to great lengths to hide assets[2], making sure that they are conveniently unavailable when it comes time to negotiate a settlement agreement. If you're separated for years, he can use that time to his advantage. For example, he might sell his boat to a friend for next to nothing with the understanding that he'll buy it back right after the divorce is final.

A long separation without a legal separation agreement can affect your eventual settlement.

If your husband loses his job, becomes ill, goes on disability, or experiences other changes in his circumstances during your prolonged separation, the amount of alimony and/or child support you could expect to receive could be significantly reduced.

Of course, your own circumstances could change, as well. You may be forced to lower your living standards during a long separation. The longer you make do with less, the harder it will be to convince a judge that your alimony should be calculated based on your previous marital lifestyle.

The legal environment for your eventual divorce could change during a prolonged separation.

Any number of legal complications can arise if you and your husband stay separated indefinitely without an agreement. What if your husband moves out of state? Laws governing virtually all aspects of the divorce process vary significantly from one state to another, and many states have recently passed severe limitations on the amount and duration of alimony that judges can award. A long separation can give your husband plenty of time to establish residency in a state which has enacted such laws (most states only require 6-12 months' residency before filing for divorce), and given the enthusiasm for alimony "reform"[3] currently sweeping the nation, your husband might not even have to move in order to find alimony laws more favorable to him. (Check what's going on in your own state legislature. As I discuss in Chapter 30, most of the recent changes to alimony laws have not been good news for divorcing women.) Even worse, he could move overseas, in which case legal tangles become potential nightmares.

Absence may make his heart (or yours) grow fonder . . . for someone else.

Meeting someone new should be good news for a happy, fulfilling future, but entering into a new relationship while you are still legally married might jeopardize your standing in divorce settlement negotiations. In addition, in some states, adultery (which is defined legally as having a sexual relationship with a person who is not your spouse) could negatively impact child custody and your ability to receive alimony, too. What's more, if your husband is in a new relationship, he might be dissipating marital assets by buying her gifts, taking her to expensive restaurants and on luxury vacations, or actually paying her living expenses!

Silence may be golden, but it's potentially very expensive.

You and your husband may have begun your separation with all good intentions to keep the communication channels open and do right by each other. In most cases, I'm sorry to say, this phase doesn't last long. Whether it results from disinterest or active animosity, as a separation drags on, communication with an estranged spouse can easily and often break down entirely. If you are financially dependent on your husband and don't have a legal separation agreement in place, you have nothing to fall back on if he stops sending checks and won't take your calls.

What's the solution?

If you're going to be separated for longer than a short trial period, I urge you to meet with a divorce attorney and have a legal separation agreement drawn up (assuming your state allows for legal separations—not all states do). At a minimum, the agreement should cover who pays for what while you are separated, and who is responsible for which debts. Make sure it ensures you have access to liquid assets and provides indemnification from or limited liability for debts incurred by your husband.

Think of the separation agreement as a precursor to your divorce agreement. (Indeed, a well-drafted separation agreement covers virtually all of the same ground, including the division of assets and debts, alimony, child support, etc.). Making it as specific, comprehensive, and protective as possible can save you negotiation hassles down the road, while helping to ensure both short- and long-term financial security.

As Marilyn B. Chinitz[4], Esq., Partner at the New York law firm Blank Rome LLP, explained, a legal separation agreement can also help you mitigate some financial risk.

"Although separating certainly can have benefits, living apart from your spouse without a formal written separation agreement can put you at risk. If you separate, you still remain liable for your spouse's debts and legal issues, in which they are involved notwithstanding the fact that you are not living together," she told me. "A written separation agreement would appropriately address those issues providing for indemnification, for example, or limiting your liability for debts incurred by your spouse during the separation. If your spouse fails to pay certain marital debt, because you are still married although not living together, the creditor can seek remedies against you for the joint debts. Informal separations without a document detailing the terms of your separation, that is, how you will share the marital assets, what do you do about joint credit cards, who pays maintenance, and how you will distribute assets acquired during the separation, can cause difficulties down the road leading to litigation."

Attorney Chinitz, who has represented both Tom Cruise and Michael Douglas, also stressed that a written separation agreement can help ensure your fair share of marital assets.

"Indeed, as time goes on, communication and cooperation with your estranged spouse may no longer exist. Your agreement should give you ready access to liquid assets—you may need these assets to pay bills," she said. "Most importantly, if you separate without an agreement, you may not receive your share of the marital assets acquired, which may be depleted or lost because you were unaware of how your estranged spouse was managing the funds or marital business."

So, once you have a comprehensive legal separation agreement in place, which is better financially: remaining legally separated or divorce?

It depends. In a few limited and specific circumstances, a well-defined legal separation can represent a better financial strategy than divorce. Otherwise, there's very little difference between the two—unless you or your ex plan to remarry. Here are a handful of key questions you need to mull over as you decide if and when it's time to end your legal separation and finalize your divorce:

» **Have you met the 10-year requirement for social security benefits[5]?**

If a marriage has lasted at least 10 years, a divorced spouse who has not remarried is entitled at age 62 (with various other requirements) to social security benefits equal to the greater of: 1) those based on her (assuming she is the lesser earning person) own work record or 2) 50 percent of what her ex-husband is entitled to based on his work record. Because of this law, many people who have been married for seven or eight years will legally separate until they cross the 10-year threshold—then, they get divorced.

Please note: The amount of your social security benefits will be reduced if you opt to take them prior to your normal retirement date. So, although you may be eligible to start receiving benefits at age 62, depending on your circumstances, you may want to delay doing so until your normal retirement age or beyond. You can actually receive more for each year you delay post-retirement age up until age 70.

» **Will you be able to continue receiving health insurance benefits under your husband's plan? Will he be able to continue receiving health insurance benefits under yours?**

Naturally, once a couple is divorced, most employer health plans will no longer cover the employee's ex-spouse. Remaining legally separated, but not divorcing, may solve that problem, although you'll have to carefully check the fine print in your employment benefit packages to know for sure. Some employers view a legal separation the same as a divorce and will deny benefits accordingly. (Note: Some people (particularly those with what could be deemed "pre-existing conditions") used to remain legally separated so they could stay on their spouse's health plan. Under the Affordable Care Act—commonly known as "ObamaCare"—pre-existing conditions are no longer a factor in determining eligibility for healthcare. Even so, you might not want to change health insurance plans or doctors, if you don't have to.)

» **Is there a tax benefit to you if you file jointly?**

Many couples assume they will save money by filing joint tax returns, so they legally separate but do not divorce in order to preserve that right. In addition, there also may be estate-planning implications. However, please don't let *assumptions* like these lead you into trouble. Federal tax law in this area is quite complex, and then it becomes even more so, because the IRS usually follows state law for determining marital status. *In other words, whether or not you are considered married or unmarried will depend upon complicated laws at both the state and federal levels.*

For example, according to tax law[6], an individual legally separated from his or her spouse under a decree of divorce or a decree of separate maintenance shall not be considered married. But, not every state allows for a decree of separate maintenance; if you live in one of those states, you are still considered married until your divorce is final. You need to ask your attorney and/or tax advisor whether your current legal status meets the definition of a decree of separate maintenance.

» **How will divorcing impact your eligibility for military benefits?**
Similar to social security benefits, military pension benefits also have a 10-year marriage requirement for ex-spouses to be eligible to collect. In addition, there is a 20-year marriage requirement for an ex-spouse to retain PX and Commissary shopping privileges after divorce.

» **Is pooling resources the only way you can maintain a certain lifestyle?**
For some couples, maintaining two separate

households is simply too expensive. Some decide to divide their home into "his" and "her" areas, so they can maintain a certain lifestyle (albeit one that's now separate). However, a decision to pool certain resources is not *necessarily* straightforward. In the case of alimony, for example, the IRS maintains that "spouses cannot be members of the same household. Payments to your spouse while you are members of the same household are not alimony if you are legally separated under a decree of divorce or separate maintenance. A home you formerly shared is considered one household, even if you physically separate yourselves in the home. You are not treated as members of the same household if one of you is preparing to leave the household and does leave no later than one month after the date of the payment." In other words, alimony would not be tax deductible by the payor, if they are living in the same household.

» **Do either of you have a religious or moral objection to divorce?**
Some couples choose to remain separated for religious or moral reasons. If you or your husband come from a religious background that frowns upon divorce, separating, but not divorcing, may be the "ideal" solution for you.

» **Would you (or he) like to remarry?**
Don't forget: Neither of you can remarry until your divorce is finalized.

The decision to remain legally separated rather than divorce can be quite complex. Weigh your options carefully and consult with qualified divorce professionals so you can make smart choices, ones that will help keep you financially secure, prevent long-term separation limbo and help you decide if and when it's time to end your legal separation and finalize your divorce.

"If it's Splitsville, do it wisely and make certain you safeguard your assets and property, protecting yourself for the future," Attorney Chinitz advised.

Reminder: While it may not be your first inclination, and it can be difficult with so much going on, I urge you to *Think Financially, Not Emotionally*®7 about ending your marriage. "Divorce" can seem like an ugly word, but what it really signifies is a new beginning—and to establish the best possible footing for the rest of your life, you need to focus on the financial aspects now.

Hot tip: While a legal separation governed by a written agreement is much, much better than long-term separation limbo without an agreement, there are only some limited, specific circumstances under which a well-defined legal separation can represent a better financial strategy than divorce. Discuss your situation with your attorney and divorce financial advisor to be sure you understand where you stand regarding social security, military benefits, tax implications, health insurance, and the like, as outlined above.

Legal matters: If you are going to live apart from your husband beyond a reasonable trial period, then you should obtain a legal separation agreement, provided that's an available option in your state. No matter how separate your day-to-day lives become, unless you're divorced, you're still legally married, with all the liabilities that implies. (And remember: Neither one of you can remarry until your divorce is finalized.) If you don't have a legal separation agreement stating otherwise, and your husband is sued, engages in fraud, or finagles joint tax returns, your assets might very well also be at risk. Consult a divorce attorney in your state about drawing up a legal separation agreement to protect yourself. Some states require such an agreement before you can file for divorce; others recognize but do not require them; still others don't recognize them at all.

CHAPTER 2

WHY YOU MIGHT WANT TO KEEP A SECRET FUND IN CASE YOU DIVORCE

I always advise women, happily married or otherwise, to be aware of and take an active role in their family's finances. For example, a wife needs to know how much her husband earns (including bonuses, commissions, restricted stock/stock options, and other perks), especially if he has a cash-based business[1] or professional practice.

Above and beyond that, though, women who come to my office for help with the financial aspects of their divorces tend to have one regret in common: that they didn't maintain more control over their *own* money during their marriages.

Fortunately, if you're married—and even if you're in the process of divorcing—it's never too late to begin being more financially independent . . . and even small steps can make a big difference. For instance, I encourage all women to maintain a separate bank account, one that your husband has no access to and maybe doesn't even know about.

You need to have money that your husband can't access or control.

Having money that's exclusively yours can be very powerful emotionally, as well as financially. These days, many women are years into lucrative careers when they marry. If you gave up paid work to devote time to parenting and household management, however happy a decision that was, you may have taken a significant blow to your well-earned independence and self-determination. Maintaining a financial reserve of your own can help alleviate that sense of loss.

What's more, if you sense that divorce is anywhere on the horizon, it can be critically important for you to have a source of funds that your husband cannot access. For starters, you'll want money available to spend on your own team of divorce professionals, and your husband should have no say in your choice.

I hear far too many horror stories about husbands who clean out joint accounts, leaving their wives little or no money to hire attorneys and other divorce professionals[2]. This is especially dangerous when dealing with a narcissist[3] and/or an abuser, who will have no qualms at all about running up divorce expenses ad infinitum just because he knows you won't be able to keep up. Maintaining your own financial reserves can thwart this tactic early on.

Should your funds be secret?

Every woman has to decide the answer to that question for herself. Maintaining a secret fund that belongs only to you can be empowering in a way that actually strengthens your marriage. Think of it this way: If keeping a secret fund makes you feel less anxious about financial matters, you may find it alleviates tensions many other couples find insurmountable. Or, maybe your husband decides to invest heavily in something you don't believe in, or wants to donate substantially to a cause you don't support. Knowing there is money (secret or not) that only you control, may help you maintain a healthy perspective based on how *you* choose to invest, donate, spend, etc.

On the other hand, keeping secrets in a marriage can create trouble. Your private bank account should not be intended to cause an erosion of trust in your relationship, and I encourage you to think about it carefully (and maybe even discuss it *before* you get married[4]).

Keep in mind that your private financial reserve doesn't *have* to be secret; it could simply be funded with separate, that is, non-marital, assets. Let's not forget that women, particularly those who marry later, often bring significant amounts of separate property into their marriages. With the right planning, through premarital protective measures (prenups, trusts, etc.)[5], these assets can remain separate and provide a measure of security and assurance. Even after they're married, some women use postnups as a way to protect themselves financially if the marriage fails and they aren't able to pick up their careers from where they left off.

Don't risk being accused of hiding assets.

I've written before about the consequences of hiding assets[6] during divorce. I've called it unethical, underhanded, shady, deplorable, and most importantly, illegal . . . and it is. While having an account in your own name for your own use is not **at all** the same thing as hiding assets so they can't become part of a divorce settlement agreement, you want to be very careful not to cross that line.

Furthermore, if you use a secret account to fund expensive separate vacations, clothing, hobbies, an affair, etc., you may be charged with dissipation of the marital estate.

So, how much money should it be?

When asked, "How much money should I keep in my secret fund?" my answer is always, "It depends." If you need to divorce a narcissist and/or abuser, or face what could be a protracted custody battle[7], you might require tens or even hundreds of thousands of dollars. Naturally, that would be difficult to accumulate under most circumstances, but several of my clients were able to survive and defend their rights because of a large inheritance that, fortunately, they kept as separate property. Whatever amount of money you put into your secret account, the inner knowledge that you can take care of yourself, at least to some extent, could prove priceless.

To my mind, the advantages of maintaining a secret fund often outweigh the potential pitfalls. I see every day how important it is for women to retain at least some degree of financial independence within their marriages. It's a perfect example of how important it is to *Think Financially, Not Emotionally*®[8] well before your marriage runs into trouble . . . or even if it never does.

Reminder: Don't let a secret fund damage your credibility in a divorce proceeding. If you keep a secret account in case of divorce, use it judiciously.

Hot tip: For your separate fund, especially if you've chosen to keep its existence to yourself, you should use a bank other than the one(s) where you and your husband have other accounts. Arrange to have your statements delivered electronically to a private email address, so you won't have to conceal postal mail delivered to your home.

Legal matters: Remember that you'll have to disclose all of your accounts, secret or otherwise, on the Financial Affidavit[9] that's part of your divorce proceedings. And, if the money in that secret account was not separate property (e.g. premarital, from an inheritance) and was accumulated during the marriage, then it is still marital property[10], and will be divided accordingly.

CHAPTER 3

DISINHERITING YOUR HUSBAND: WHY, WHEN, AND HOW

If you are contemplating divorce, there is plenty you can do to prepare. Ideally, you will be interviewing and hiring your attorney and divorce financial advisor, researching the laws of your state, setting aside funds, obtaining and securing copies of legal and financial documents, and otherwise getting all your proverbial ducks in a row. To ensure the best possible outcome, you want to be well-informed, well-prepared, and well-financed.

Disinheriting your husband, to the extent possible while you are still legally married, is an important part of this process, and yet many women overlook it. While there is no way to know how long your divorce will take—some contentious and financially complex divorces can drag on for years — it is safe to say that there will be significant time between the decision to legally dissolve your marriage and the day that your divorce is final. It is worth your while to ensure that should anything happen to you during that interval, your husband doesn't benefit more than legally necessary.

Why is it so important to disinherit your husband?

People often leave most or all of their assets to their spouse. Since you were wed, you have likely named your husband as the primary or sole beneficiary of your will, as well as 401(k)s, IRAs, insurance policies, and other legal and financial arrangements that have been made during your marriage.

Now that you're getting divorced, do you really want your soon-to-be-ex to inherit all of your assets? In most cases, I'd guess absolutely not! However, if you die before your divorce is final—or in some states, before a legal separation agreement[1] has been signed by both parties—this is exactly what will happen.

It could be even worse. Imagine that your husband inherits all your property under the terms of your current will, then remarries, and leaves all of it to his new wife and their kids. By not changing your will, you could unintentionally disinherit your own children!

Can you disinherit him before the divorce?

In most states, you cannot completely disinherit your husband while you're legally married, even if you've cut him out of your will. That's because of a legal provision called "elective share," which originated to prevent surviving spouses from becoming a financial burden on the state.

Briefly, elective share provides that, while you are still married, your spouse will inherit some percentage of your estate, even if you have specified that he should not. (You will not be surprised to learn it is also called "forced share.")

In most jurisdictions, the elective share is one-third to one-half of the estate. While I'm sure you'd prefer he gets nothing, a third or half is certainly much better than 100%. And of course, the moment your divorce is finalized, you can and should rewrite your will to disinherit him completely.

It may be possible for you and your husband to negotiate a separation agreement which provides that each of you gives up all claims to the other's estate. Once again, state laws differ greatly; consult with both your divorce attorney and a trust and estate attorney licensed in your jurisdiction.

What should you do before the divorce gets underway?

Ideally, you should change your will and all your other estate planning documents before filing for divorce.

Don't forget to update your living will (medical directives) and financial power of attorney, so that someone you trust has the ability to make medical and/or financial decisions on your behalf should you become incapacitated. (Do you really want your soon-to-be-ex-husband making possible life and death decisions for you at this point in your relationship?)

You may also want to name new beneficiaries on your life insurance policies, retirement accounts, annuities and other investments where applicable. If beneficiary changes to some accounts such as 401(k)s and pension plans require the consent of your spouse, then in all likelihood, you will not be able to change them until after your divorce has been finalized. But do make what changes you can.

Note that once formal divorce proceedings have begun, you might not be legally able to change or move accounts, name new beneficiaries, and/or revise other legal and financial agreements. Many states enforce what's known as an Automatic Temporary Restraining Order (ATRO)[2] to ensure that both parties' assets and ownership interests remain unchanged until they have been divided according to the final divorce settlement agreement.

What happens after the divorce is final?

After the divorce is final (congratulations!), you are free to update, revoke, and amend your estate planning documents and beneficiary designations as you see fit.

In some states, your ex-husband may automatically be removed from your will after your divorce is finalized. Even so, it is still a good idea to formally remove him by revising or rewriting your will. In any event, because beneficiary designations supersede the terms of your will, *you must change those beneficiary designations as soon as you legally can,* to make sure that your ex-husband is no longer your beneficiary on life insurance policies, retirement accounts, pensions, wills, trusts, and annuities. Review these items very carefully and consult with a trust and estate attorney who will prepare the required documents and coordinate the timing and recording of the changes.

Reminder: Even though you can't totally disinherit your husband before your divorce is final, don't neglect to change the beneficiaries on your insurance policies, retirement plans, etc. as soon as you know you'll be divorcing. You might otherwise have to wait until after the divorce.

Hot tip: Whether or not you think your divorce is likely to be contentious, it is wise to make copies of all relevant legal and financial documents in advance. Keep them with a trusted friend or in a secure place your husband can't access. Then, once your divorce is underway, if things get ugly, you won't waste time and burn through legal fees trying to obtain documents in his possession.

Legal matters: Elective share laws vary widely in their details. Some states require that the marriage be of a minimum duration before elective share can be invoked. Others have special provisions if there are children from the marriage. Some states specify that if a spouse invokes elective share, then he is forbidden from taking anything else from the estate. It is critical that you consult an estate planning attorney who knows the laws where you live.

CHAPTER 4

WHAT YOU CAN AND CANNOT WITHDRAW FROM JOINT ACCOUNTS

Reaching the decision to file for divorce can be a long, painful, and emotionally draining process. However, as soon as you conclude that it's what you need to do (or if you believe your husband may be about to file), you need to think calmly and clearly about securing the funds to hire a professional divorce team[1]. You will also need to cover your living expenses until an interim arrangement or a final settlement agreement is reached.

If you don't have a significant income stream of your own or a substantial secret fund as I discussed in the previous chapter, finding the money to get through the divorce process can be a difficult problem—even for affluent women. As a result, you may be wondering about withdrawing money from the joint account(s) you and your husband use to pay household bills. Can you use a joint account to set aside funds for your own upcoming needs? *Should* you? If so, how much should you withdraw? What can you do if you have limited funds and can't access your marital assets?

I asked several respected divorce attorneys from around the country to weigh in on these critical questions, and as you might imagine, there are nuances and legal implications for every scenario. Here are my questions and how the experts responded:

Is it a good idea to take money from joint accounts to use for my own expenses?

Marilyn B. Chinitz[2], Esq., Partner at the New York law firm Blank Rome LLP, said it is. "Clients have a right to one-half of the value of the jointly titled funds and should access those monies to secure funds should they later be closed out of accounts held by the other spouse," explained Attorney Chinitz, whose clients include Michael Douglas and Tom Cruise. "If there is one joint account and the monied spouse has multiple accounts in their sole name to which the non-monied spouse has no access, it may be appropriate for the non-monied spouse to secure as much money as they can to ensure that they are not left out in the cold."

Chicago attorney Debra DiMaggio[3], Esq., Principal of the Law Offices of Debra DiMaggio, sees two ways to answer the question. Her advice would be not to withdraw money from joint accounts if the withdrawal itself could spur divorce proceedings. "On the other hand, if the divorce was inevitable and the couple would most likely have been engaged in a difficult and acrimonious divorce anyway, then the answer is, 'Yes.' But even then, a rule of reason has to prevail with the funds earmarked to pay an attorney retainer and pay routine bills until a temporary court order can be secured," Attorney DiMaggio said. "I'd rarely recommend withdrawing 50% of the account balance. The account balance might be temporarily inflated in anticipation of paying property taxes or income taxes and a withdrawal of half might divest the ability to pay."

When is the best time to withdraw funds from joint accounts?

Once a divorce is initiated, withdrawals from joint accounts in many states are legally restricted through an Automatic Temporary Restraining Order (ATRO), a court order prohibiting either spouse from making certain financial changes once a divorce action begins. (To learn more, read Volume I, Chapter 21.) Since this is the case in New York, Attorney Chinitz cautioned that any such withdrawals there can only be done *before* legal action has formally begun.

A similar restriction exists in California, reported Laura A. Wasser[4], Esq., Partner in the Los Angeles family law firm of Wasser, Cooperman & Carter and author of the book, *It Doesn't Have to Be That Way: How to Divorce Without Destroying Your Family or Bankrupting Yourself*. Attorney Wasser acknowledged that funds can be withdrawn prior to the filing and service of a petition for divorce, but warned that doing so poses its own risk.

"This could very well start the case off in the wrong way, as husband would feel that she was divorce planning and seek vengeance," said Attorney Wasser, whose client list includes Maria Shriver, Heidi Klum, Angelina Jolie, Christina Aguilera, Britney Spears, and many others. "I generally recommend an advance distribution of funds at the outset of a case if my client feels that maintaining expenses will be difficult during the pendency of the proceeding. Obviously a lot depends on the parties and their respective personalities."

How much can I withdraw?

Suppose you and your spouse have a joint account containing $400,000. Is it fair to assume you're entitled to half of it? What if you know the $400,000 represents just a small portion of your total marital assets, but this is the only account you can access. Can you then justifiably take out more, or all, of the $400,000?

According to Los Angeles divorce attorney and Avvo.com legal analyst Kelly Chang Rickert[6], Esq., of the Law Offices of Kelly Chang, "prior to any divorce papers being filed, you can withdraw any amount you'd like." After papers are filed, withdrawals may be more restricted. "Technically, if it's community [property], then you can withdraw up to 50%," she explained. "The problem is, the other spouse may have reimbursement claims, etc., and because there is a restraining order, you may run into problems if you have a vindictive ex." Attorney Chang Rickert's ultimate recommendation is to withdraw any and all funds you deem necessary *prior* to filing a divorce. "That way you don't run into any problems with violating court orders and such," she said.

One approach to the joint account is to try talking with your spouse about splitting it, suggested Jennifer Brandt[7], Esq., Philadelphia divorce attorney, Avvo. com legal analyst, and partner at Cozen O'Connor. "I typically advise clients to speak with their spouse about closing the account and equally dividing the monies. If that is not possible and they cannot communicate with their spouse, they should take no more than 50% of the money. The reason for this is that usually they will be entitled to no less than this amount in the divorce," she said.

What if the spouse has significant funds of his own, and the joint account represents a small percentage of total marital assets? Would that warrant withdrawing more than half the joint account balance?

"I don't advise a client to take any more than 50% even if the spouse has additional funds solely in his name because this just usually leads to a money grab on his part which, in the long run, can make the divorce even more complex," Attorney Brandt continued. "If a client needs additional monies to fund the litigation, I would advise that she petition the court and get them by way of court order."

Unfortunately, even retaining an attorney to file the necessary motion for a court order can be a prohibitive expense for a woman whose husband has cleaned out the joint accounts ahead of her.

Is there any reason I should *not* withdraw money from joint accounts?

Bari Z. Weinberger[8], Esq., owner and managing partner of the Weinberger Law Group, a firm exclusively devoted to family law in New Jersey, generally does not recommend her clients remove any money from joint accounts. "Inevitably, even if the client is acting merely to safeguard some funds for security purposes, the other spouse will interpret it as an initiative to liquidate and dissipate assets and act in kind," she explained. "Then the game playing begins. Before you know it, both parties are tapping into every resource they can find, hiding money and jewelry, removing items from the home and what started out as a simple plan to protect a joint account has spiraled way out of control. Litigation will erupt and the parties will spend mountains of money on their lawyers to have to deal it through the courts, likely branding both parties as manipulators to the judge."

Like Attorney Brandt, Attorney Weinberger prefers to communicate from the beginning. "Discuss with the other party the desire to each have access to joint funds and to split certain assets," she said. "If the other side refuses, there is always the option of asking the judge to allow freedom and access to certain accounts throughout the pending litigation so that one side does not have the upper hand in maintaining control of all of the finances. Judges appreciate this method and approach as opposed to the former. I absolutely believe that both parties should be on an equal playing field throughout the case. However, it is imperative to be forward thinking and proceed with caution before recommending certain courses of action to a client that *could* create an unnecessary level of fear and suspicion in the other party, thereby spawning a nightmare of events for your client whose only goal was some peace of mind and security."

Although I agree with those views in theory, I've seen far too many situations in which the woman, hoping for a non-contentious divorce, attempts to play nicely and by the rules, only to get "screwed" when her husband then cleans out all their accounts. This leaves a woman without a significant source of income in dire straits. It's especially dangerous when dealing with a narcissistic[9] and/or abusive husband, who will use this as a tactic and then do everything possible to drive up her legal costs so that she quickly runs out of money.

In my experience, withdrawing funds from joint accounts, unless and until restricted by an ATRO, is a wise, self-protective measure for a divorcing woman with no income of her own. After all, as Attorney Chang Rickert said, "All is fair in love and war." Your husband will certainly be thinking along those lines. Of course you'll need to consult your own attorney with the specifics of your case, but my advice is to *Think Financially, Not Emotionally*®10 and take every step you can to protect yourself.

Reminder: If you do withdraw funds from joint accounts, make sure that they are used judiciously to cover your expenses during the divorce. This is not the time for extravagant purchases or luxury travel (or revenge spending). You need to be able to demonstrate that you are living sensibly. Don't give your husband any reason to claim otherwise.

Hot tip: When you set aside funds for your own use, deposit them with a different bank than the one that your husband uses or that the two of you used for joint accounts. Choosing a new bank is cleaner for record-keeping, emphasizes the new separateness of your finances from his, and prevents any of your information being unintentionally revealed to him by a well-meaning bank employee who knows you both, but may not be aware that you're divorcing.

Legal matters: Don't assume your accounts and policies will "automatically" be notified that an Automatic Temporary Restraining Order (ATRO) is in effect. For instance, in states where an ATRO prohibits the modification of beneficiaries, you need to inform your bank, stock brokerage, insurance companies, etc. about the divorce action. The courts will not take care of this important step; notifying your bank, etc. is *your* responsibility!

CHAPTER 5

SHOULD YOU MOVE OUT OF THE MARITAL HOME? HERE'S WHAT THE EXPERTS SAY

When you're going through divorce, it may be tempting to compare your situation to celebrities who are going through the same kind of turmoil. Ashton and Demi[1], Arnold and Maria[2], Tiger and Elin, Katie and Tom, Heidi and Seal . . . It's easy to come up with a list of high-profile divorces that have grabbed headlines—not just on celebrity gossip websites, but even in more mainstream news. While I'll agree that articles like these can provide food for thought (and maybe even make you feel a little better about *your* circumstances), I also have to offer a few words of caution: If you feel yourself drawn to these stories, please take them with a grain of salt. Why? Because celebrity divorce "news" can be a source of misinformation.

Case in point: In 2013, the entertainment headlines proclaimed there was a wrinkle in the ongoing divorce of Bethenny Frankel and Jason Hoppy, of reality TV fame. Frankel, the force behind Skinnygirl, and Hoppy, a pharmaceutical sales rep, filed for divorce in January 2013, but reportedly, they remained living together in the $5M Tribeca loft apartment they moved into during presumably happier days.

According to one article[3], "neither Bethenny nor Jason is willing to move out of the apartment because if one of them does it can be construed as abandonment in New York State. If one or the other abandons the home it makes it all the more difficult for the one who leaves to make a claim on the property in a divorce settlement." However, that's simply not true!

As it turns out, this is a shining example of why not to take divorce advice from entertainment news—and I consulted several divorce attorneys to confirm my take on this. Essentially, we all agree that if Bethenny and Jason's New York apartment was acquired during their marriage, and with marital assets, it would be considered marital property[4]. As such, the value of the property would be subject to division in the divorce settlement regardless of who was actually living there.

"The apartment remains a marital asset subject to distribution regardless of who lives there," Judith L.

Poller[5], Esq., Partner at Pryor Cashman in New York City, told me. "The law used to be before no-fault divorce was enacted that leaving a residence could result in a ground for 'abandonment' being able to be asserted. But that law changed in 2010."

Bari Z. Weinberger[6], Esq., owner and managing partner of the Weinberger Law Group, a law firm exclusively devoted to family law in New Jersey, agreed. "In NJ, if the property is marital then both parties have equal rights to buy-out the other's share and if both make that claim, it will be sold with the net realized proceeds of sale divided," she said. "It makes no difference which party remained in the home during the divorce process."

If we dig a little deeper, there are even more lessons divorcing women can learn from the Frankel-Hoppy divorce:

Regardless of whether or not someone moves out, you'll need to come to terms about financial obligations for upkeep of the property. How (and why) Bethenny was willing to endure the emotional stress and strife of sharing an apartment with her soon-to-be-ex on a day-to-day basis when she could afford to move to an equally luxurious setting elsewhere baffles me. Most women, if they can afford it, choose to live apart from their husbands during the divorce process, but as Laura A. Wasser[7], Esq., Partner in the family law firm of Wasser, Cooperman & Carter and author of *It Doesn't Have to Be That*

Way: How to Divorce Without Destroying Your Family or Bankrupting Yourself, explained, it's not as simple as packing an overnight bag and checking out.

"There should be some serious discussions about 1) the property itself; care, maintenance, interim financial obligations, etc., 2) items left in the property (one does not give up his/her right to art, furniture, appliances, etc., and these items will be discussed, divided and retrieved later in the proceeding), and 3) boundaries (if the property is owned jointly and one party moves out, does the other have exclusive use and possession and an expectation of privacy, or will the 'out-spouse' be entitled to have some use and enjoyment even after his/her departure?)," Attorney Wasser said.

In short, the parties have to agree on the terms of the move out. "Unless a judge makes an order kicking one party out and specifies exclusive use and possession it is up to them to stipulate their intent," added Attorney Wasser, whose client list includes Maria Shriver, Heidi Klum, Angelina Jolie, Christina Aguilera, Britney Spears, and many others.

Leaving the marital residence may affect your claim of wanting to be the custodial parent. For many couples, child custody is the most important issue of all, and at times, concerns over child custody can keep both parents living—however awkwardly—in the same home. In fact, this may have been the biggest factor in play in the Frankel-Hoppy case.

Bethenny and Jason have a daughter, Bryn, and both parents reportedly filed for primary custody.

"If either party leaves, that may affect his/her claims of wanting to be the custodial parent," Attorney Poller said. "It is certainly an important issue, however, with respect to custody of a child or children. Until there is a parenting plan in place, if the parties are interested in maintaining a meaningful relationship in the child's life, 'abandonment' prior to an agreement being entered into, may indicate a lack of real interest in the child's daily life. In addition, from a purely leverage standpoint, if one party moves out, it may slow down the process of coming to a resolution of the matter because the tension and the immediacy of physically separating is not as paramount."

Likewise, Attorney Weinberger generally advises clients with custody disputes to stay at home.

"I generally suggest to my clients **NOT** to leave the home if there is a custody dispute because leaving can create a new 'primary residential parent' by default, and if the process takes an extended period of time it sort of creates a new status quo. It can certainly be overcome . . . but it's preferable to remain in the home," she explained. "I also suggest to my clients to remain in the home together if possible because the person who leaves may still have financial obligations to contribute toward the expenses of the home while at the same time having to make payments for the new home. It can be costly and prohibitive over time, and we know that the process can be extensive."

However, concerns about custody can be resolved in a variety of ways. For instance, if you were to move out, your attorney could argue that you are doing so in order to reduce ongoing marital strife out of concern for your child(ren)'s emotional well-being during the divorce proceedings. You can also establish interim custody.

"One way of effectuating a move of one spouse or the other is to create an interim custody schedule which ensures that even after he or she has left the family residence there will still be frequent and continuous access to the minor children," Attorney Wasser said. "By doing this the parents establish both security and a precedent for ongoing custody."

If both of you remain in the marital residence, there may be more incentive to proceed towards a final divorce settlement agreement. "I like when my client remains in the home if my client is under court obligation to pay temporary support during the process," Attorney Weinberger said. "Why? If my client leaves then the other party has little if any incentive to negotiate a final settlement because that person is sitting pretty at home (possibly with the kids) and has the bills paid with support. There is no reason to settle. If both parties continue to live in the home, it is usually uncomfortable for everyone and the emotions catch up to create a strong desire to get the matter concluded in final settlement and compromises happen as a result."

As you can see, deciding to leave the marital home can be quite complex—even if you're not a celebrity. Please keep in mind that laws about many aspects of divorce vary widely from state to state[9], and the attorney quotes above are applicable to the laws in the state where they practice, namely, California, New Jersey, and New York. Be sure to consult with a divorce attorney in your state to learn what is applicable to your case, and as always, weigh all of your options carefully.

Reminder: If your home was acquired during your marriage, and with marital assets, it is considered marital property. Most marital residences are significant assets, and if the marital residence is marital property, it will be subject to division in the divorce settlement regardless of who is actually living there during the divorce proceedings.

Hot tip: As always, your safety is of the utmost importance. If you're involved in a physically and/or mentally abusive marriage, please seek help. There are community-based organizations, private counselors, therapists, and other professionals who can offer the immediate assistance you need. They'll help you create a plan that will keep you and your children safe, whether that's in your marital residence or another location.

Legal matters: In a Community Property State, both spouses are typically considered equal owners of all marital property. In other words, if you live in a Community Property State, whatever you earn or acquire during the marriage is co-owned by both parties, regardless of who earned it or whose name is on the title. That means whatever you earn or acquire during the marriage is split 50-50 during a divorce.

If you live in an Equitable Distribution State, the law "sees" assets somewhat differently. In an Equitable Distribution State, if your name appears on an asset (e.g., the deed to a house or the title to a car), you are considered the owner. However, in an Equitable Distribution State, your spouse has the legal right to claim a fair and equitable portion of those assets in a divorce.

There are nine Community Property States: Arizona, California, Idaho, Louisiana, Nevada, New Mexico, Texas, Washington, and Wisconsin. Couples living in Alaska can "opt in" for community property, and Puerto Rico is a community property jurisdiction. The remaining 41 states are known as Equitable Distribution States (or Common Law States).

CHAPTER 6

WHEN TO FILE FOR DIVORCE: WHAT BEING PREPARED REALLY MEANS

Although I work with women at every stage of the divorce process, many of my clients schedule their initial consultation early on, when they first start to think about filing. They want to know how the divorce will impact them financially and what their chances are of having a secure financial future.

Once we get down to the details, this one question always arises: When is the best time to file?

Over the years I've observed that some women have very specific ideas about when the "right" time will be. Some want to wait until they feel certain they've exhausted every possibility of reconciliation. Others want the holidays to be behind them or for a family birthday to pass. Some prefer to wait until the kids get out of school; others want their kids to get back to school. They want to wait until after some travel that's already been planned. Or for the New Year. Or the summer solstice.

Now, I understand the inclination to put things off until some "just right" moment. It's perfectly natural to feel reluctant to begin an unpleasant process—and unfortunately, many women know they are in for a prolonged, potentially ugly fight. I'm not at all surprised that they're reluctant to take that first, tangible, irretrievable step.

That said, I can bet your reasons for determining the right time might be widely different from mine. Here's why: In my view, if you aren't properly prepared, it's the wrong time to file, period, even if all the other circumstances you can think of are beautifully aligned. Conversely, if you are properly prepared, there is probably never going to be a "better" time.

What does "properly prepared" mean, exactly? Think of it as four corners to a foundation:

1. Your financial paperwork is in order.

Among other things, divorce will mean a more detailed examination of your finances than you have likely ever conducted during your marriage. If you have the necessary financial and legal documents on hand early in the process, you will save untold expense and unpleasantness trying to get copies of them later.

Use my <u>Divorce Financial Checklist</u> (See Appendix A)[1] to see what documents you should gather and copy. You may have items to add to the list, as well. The more you think about it, the more will occur to you. Some of these papers may concern things you haven't even thought about, let alone laid eyes on, in years. It will take time to assemble it all, and you shouldn't expect help from your husband.

2. **Your credit rating is good, and you have your own bank accounts.**

   Credit is one of those things we take for granted when everything's going smoothly. It's safe to say that divorce is a sign that not everything is going smoothly—and you need to look into your individual credit rating. Good credit will be critical to your financial well-being as a single woman. These days, people rely on it for everything from loans to leases, and even for managing household expenses. Request a copy of your credit report, and correct any errors it contains.

   If you don't already have them, you should also establish bank accounts and credit cards in your own name. Credit cards are especially important, and you shouldn't put off applying for them. Particularly if you don't have income of your own, it could take time[2] to get cards in your own name. Get started now.

3. You've saved enough money to fund your divorce.

Financially complex divorces are expensive. Attorneys, divorce financial advisors, forensic accountants, valuation and vocational experts and other professionals with necessary expertise charge hundreds of dollars an hour, and require substantial retainer fees up front.

How much you will need depends on how complicated your financial situation is and how difficult your husband and his attorney try to make it. It could be tens of thousands to even hundreds of thousands of dollars—and sometimes more! Women who've managed to set aside a secret emergency fund[3] are rarely sorry they did so. It's not just the divorce you'll have to pay for; if your husband cuts you off, you'll still need to pay credit card and household bills.

4. You've begun to assemble your professional divorce team.

Interview several family/matrimonial law attorneys before you choose a competent lawyer to handle your case. If your divorce presents any unique circumstances requiring special expertise, find someone with demonstrated experience in that area.

You will also need a divorce financial advisor[4]. This person will examine every aspect of your marital finances, and work through multiple settlement scenarios to make sure you come through your divorce in optimum financial shape. The goal is not only to get the best possible settlement, but also to make it last as long as possible after your divorce.

While I urge you to *Think Financially, Not Emotionally*[®5], it isn't because I don't recognize that divorce is an intensely emotional process. That's why I recommend that a compassionate therapist[6] be part of your team. You'll need a support network to help you cope, and a therapist can be key to that.

With these four cornerstones in place, you'll be ready to file for divorce no matter what else is on your calendar. What's more, with the peace of mind that comes from being well-positioned for financial success, you'll find it easier to manage the other factors that were weighing on you as well.

Reminder: Keep your copies of financial and legal documents with a trusted friend or relative, or use a safe deposit box that your husband can't access.

Hot tip: Even if you've never paid close attention to joint credit card statements, do it now. Scrutinize every purchase. You may find that your husband has been using marital assets to buy his girlfriend expensive gifts or take her on vacation. That's something you'll want to be able to document. Even if you don't care about the girlfriend, you should absolutely care about the assets he's squandering!

Legal matters: Don't procrastinate when hiring an attorney. Waiting too long could give your husband time to "conflict out" the best lawyers in your area, making it difficult for you to retain one yourself. All he has to do is meet with each lawyer just long enough to establish an attorney-client relationship. Any attorney who has met with your husband would usually be prohibited from representing you, whether or not your husband actually hires her/him. (See Volume I, Chapter 19 for a more detailed discussion.)

CHAPTER 7

THE PROS AND CONS OF FILING FIRST

Sometimes, it pays to be first. Being first in line for concert tickets, or for any kind of sale, for that matter, usually means you'll enjoy the widest selection of available options.

On the other hand, there are times when being first may not be optimal. Do you really want to be a surgeon's inaugural patient or the first to try out new parachute equipment?

Because being first can be either a "pro" or a "con," depending on the circumstances, it's no surprise that many women have questions about how timing could affect their divorce. In the previous chapter, I discussed what you need to do to be prepared to file. Now, let's explore a related issue: timing. Are there any advantages—either legally or financially—if you are the first to file for divorce?

The answer to that question is complicated and varies from case to case. While it certainly does not make sense to race your husband to the courthouse out of mere spite or for the thin and fleeting satisfaction of winning at "gotcha," there are several legitimate reasons why you may want to file first, if you have a choice. Here is my short list of legal and financial factors you must consider before filing first:

Legal Considerations for Filing First

Filing first lets you choose where your divorce will be adjudicated. As Laura A. Wasser[1], Esq., divorce attorney to stars like Maria Shriver, Heidi Klum, Angelina Jolie, Christina Aguilera, Britney Spears, and many others, told me, filing jurisdiction can have a significant impact on virtually every issue of the divorce process.

"While in ideal circumstances couples divorce where they live, hiring lawyers or mediators whose offices are convenient for both to get to, the fact is that the filing jurisdiction will influence the outcome of every issue that may arise in the divorce proceeding—child custody, child support, spousal support, division of property," she said. "That's why it is so important to know your own state's practices concerning the key issues."

Filing first may save you from falling victim to "conflicting out." At the onset of divorce, some husbands resort to a dirty trick known as "conflicting out."[2] It happens when a husband meets for quick consultations with all the best divorce attorneys in the area, thereby rendering them unable to serve the wife because they now have an attorney-client relationship with the husband—and a "conflict of interest" with serving the wife.

Attorney Wasser explained how the process works at her firm.

"In a great many law firms—including mine —you will be routed first to a gatekeeper before an actual lawyer gets on the line. In my case, it's my secretary who runs a brief but fairly substantive screening process. She will take down basic information like your name, your spouse's name, how long you've been married, how many kids you have, where you are filing your case, and the like," she said. "The screening process runs a quick check of our database to make sure, for example, that your spouse didn't phone us a year ago and come in for a meeting in which confidential information was relayed; that would mean I couldn't represent you. Remember the famous episode of *The Sopranos* in which Tony's putative new neighbor, a slimy lawyer if ever there was one, advises him to make appointments with all the top divorce lawyers in North Jersey so Carmela won't be able to find legal representation? It worked, too; in a later episode, she freaked out at this further evidence of Tony's controlling ways. We watch out for that sort of thing in this initial screening process."

You'll learn more insights from Attorney Wasser in her book, *It Doesn't Have to Be That Way: How to*

Divorce Without Destroying Your Family or Bankrupting Yourself[3], from St. Martin's Press.

Filing first may allow you to present your case first at trial—but, testifying is one of those times when being first is not always optimal. Debra DiMaggio[4], Esq., Principal of the Law Offices of Debra DiMaggio, explained to me why the timing of a divorce litigant's testimony can be critical.

"On one hand, if you're the wronged spouse, you may feel the need to be the first to file for emotional reasons. No one wants to be the 'rejected' spouse," she said. "But on the other hand, you may not want to reveal your strategy to the other side, who can then adjust his or her presentation accordingly."

Financial Considerations of Filing First

Filing first helps you line up your divorce team. Assembling the right team of qualified experts[5] to help you achieve the best possible outcome from your divorce can take some time. You will need an excellent attorney, of course, and in financially complex divorces, it's also essential to have a qualified divorce financial advisor[6] on your side. I also recommend enlisting the help of a good therapist, as well as a vocational expert[7] if you plan to re-enter the job market.

Filing first helps gives you a jump-start on gathering all the documentation you will need before the divorce begins. It is critically important to have in your secure possession copies of all relevant financial and legal documents. These include not only bank and brokerage statements and tax returns, but also insurance policies, wills and trusts, retirement account statements, real estate records, vehicle registrations, etc. (See my Divorce Financial Checklist (See Appendix A)[8] for a comprehensive list.) Locating and copying all these documents can take considerable time and effort, particularly if your husband is controlling or secretive where finances are concerned. Filing first means that you'll have all your documentation organized and in a secure location before divorce papers are served.

Filing first may prevent your husband from hiding assets. Deplorable as it is, many husbands hide assets[9] during the divorce process. Filing first, particularly if you live in a state which requires an Automatic Temporary Restraining Order (ATRO)[10], may help guard against any underhanded tactics.

Filing first may give you an emotional edge. While I always encourage women to *Think Financially, Not Emotionally*[®11], there is an emotional component to filing first which can't be discounted. I don't need to tell you that ending a marriage can be a wrenching, heartbreaking process. Once the decision is made, though, there can be some real emotional strength to be gained from taking the first tangible steps toward your new life as a single woman. You may find that making the initial legal filing provides the psychological leg-up you sorely need, and that feeling more in control of the process will help you see the divorce through to your best advantage.

Most importantly, however, you need to build a strong, qualified divorce team[12] to guide you through the divorce proceedings and help you secure a solid financial future as an independent woman.

Reminder: Divorces are generally decided in the jurisdiction in which they are filed, and your experience and expected outcome may vary widely in different jurisdictions within the same state. State laws can be widely different regarding such crucial considerations as child custody customs and division of marital assets, including whether or not an ATRO is part of the process. Do your research, and consult with divorce attorneys wherever you might file.

Hot tip: Make sure you have access to funds and credit before you file. As soon as you think divorce is in your future (or even before[13]), begin to set aside money for the expenses involved. Make sure you have enough money to hire your divorce team; it is a critical investment in your financial future. Also, if you don't have a credit card in your own name—

and you absolutely should!—obtain one as soon as possible, as it may be more difficult to do so later.

Legal matters: Be proactive, if only for a legal consultation. "In my opinion, if a spouse senses trouble in the marriage he or she should immediately meet with an attorney to obtain information about the law and gain practical insight about the process," Attorney DiMaggio advised. "After interviewing a qualified domestic relations practitioner, that spouse will have a keener sense of his or her spouse's intentions with respect to the marriage going forward."

CHAPTER 8

THE POTENTIAL PITFALLS OF SOCIAL MEDIA, EMAIL, AND TEXTS

Social media and professional networking websites have become fundamental to how people interact in today's culture. Not only are Facebook[1], Twitter[2], Instagram[3], LinkedIn[4], and the like interactive and fun, but they're also loaded with opportunities to connect with others, either personally or professionally. There are sites for book lovers, business executives, research scientists, pilots, knitting enthusiasts . . . wherever there's an interest, there's a corner of the internet for people to socialize about it.

These days, when something happens in our lives, we post online about it to let our friends know. When something happens in our careers, we update our profiles to enhance professional connections. Often without thinking through the consequences, people share personal and professional news, triumphs and tragedies, laughs and tears . . . and lots and lots of pictures.

What does this mean for your divorce, particularly financially?

Well, first, I'm seeing that social networks and digital communications now often contribute to breakups. Second, I'm finding that they can also have unforeseen consequences in divorce settlement negotiations.

Divorce attorneys know this all too well[5]: The American Academy of Matrimonial Lawyers reports that 81% of its members have used or encountered evidence taken from social media websites. As of 2014, the majority of this evidence (66%) comes from Facebook.

Here are just a few of the ways that digital communications and social media can influence your divorce proceedings:

» **Emails and text messages can be admissible evidence in court.**

In addition to activity on social media and networking websites, emails, and texts— yes, emails and texts, the routine ways we communicate today—can sometimes be subpoenaed and examined with a fine-tooth comb.

Family lawyers advise their clients[6] not to put anything in an email, a text message, or anywhere online that they don't want the Judge to read.

» **If you think your husband may be hiding assets, social media activity might bear out your suspicions.** Your husband is probably savvy enough not to update his Facebook status to say, "I found a way to keep the boat out of the divorce!" (though I'm sure there are lawyers who could tell you that such things have actually been posted online). In less obvious ways, though, social media activity can provide important clues to hidden assets or other dirty tricks.

Married couples often have dozens of mutual friends and connections online. I've had more than one client report a steady stream of information about her estranged husband's financial activities, as relayed by mutual friends who were still following his Facebook updates. Even if he's blocked you from seeing his posts directly, you may still hear that he's taken a new girlfriend on a Caribbean sailing jaunt—a week after claiming he couldn't afford to pay spousal support.

Your husband wouldn't even have to post about his activities himself for the clues to be there. Often it is friends' online activity that reveals what the husband is up to. Maybe his pals shared pictures of their trip to Vegas in his new BMW, or his girlfriend tweeted about an expensive present after he just pleaded in court that he's broke. Or maybe a college friend of his suddenly appeared in pictures with that very boat—the one you recognize as your husband's, and suspect that this buddy is holding for him until your divorce is finalized.

You might also check to see what your husband is saying about himself on dating websites, compared to what he's saying about himself in court. Don't assume he's been smart enough to keep a low profile. His ego might overcome his better judgment.

» **Social media can pose a serious credibility problem, or worse.**

If what your husband says in legal documents is at odds with what he posts online, this can be very useful for your divorce team to know. Any discrepancies can undermine his credibility with the court. If he "checks in" (on Foursquare[7], for example) from places he denies having been, or appears to be living a lifestyle he says he can't afford, that's important information.

By referring online, even obliquely, to an impending bonus, a new job offer, or other financial circumstances he has not disclosed, your husband could raise suspicions that he is not telling the truth on his Financial

Affidavit[8]. Lying under oath is not just a credibility problem—it could have serious legal consequences.

Remember that all of the above works both ways.

Social media can definitely trip up your husband if he is hiding assets or being dishonest in other ways. But never forget that he's hoping to trip you up, as well.

If you use social media yourself, you need to exercise caution, discretion, and excellent judgment. Remember to check your privacy settings and tighten them if necessary. Even better, make sure your online conduct is unimpeachable. In social media, not every "friend" is a friend, not every follower is a supporter, and not every connection is an ally. And, unfortunately, messages you consider to be private can turn out to be anything but.

 Reminder: Every advantage that social media might give you in your divorce is an advantage it might give your husband, as well. Never post, tweet, or share *anything* online that you wouldn't say in person to the whole world, to be remembered forever.

Hot tip: If you are used to being very open about your life on social media sites, it can be a hard habit to break. Deleting posts after you've made them is not solution enough—you never know if someone has taken a screenshot of your post or picture, or if a cached version is available. Rather than navigate the social media minefield, it would be wiser and safer to deactivate your social media accounts. You can always reopen them after your divorce is final.

Legal matters: Laws about using email, texts, and social media as evidence in divorce cases are notoriously convoluted, and they also differ from state to state. Have a detailed discussion with your divorce attorney to find out what online information can be legally obtained and used in your case, and also how to protect your own privacy.

CHAPTER 9

COPING EMOTIONALLY WHILE THINKING FINANCIALLY: THE ROLE OF A THERAPIST IN YOUR DIVORCE

I write plenty about the many complex financial considerations that come into play when a couple divorces. But no matter what specific topic I explore, you'll find I consistently urge divorcing women to *Think Financially, Not Emotionally*®[1] as they negotiate their divorce financial settlement. Why? Because thinking financially helps you establish a secure financial foundation for your future as an independent single woman. By contrast, I've seen time and time again that thinking emotionally during this process leads to terrible financial decisions—and deep regrets when the consequences of these decisions become clear.

Still, there is no denying that divorce is an intensely emotional time. It can be very hard to set aside the immediate hurt, fear and anger you may be going through, even when you know it's important to concentrate on dollars and cents for the future.

So how do you cope, emotionally, while your divorce financial advisor is urging you to think financially?

For expert advice, I asked two esteemed colleagues to weigh in.

Rami Kaminski[2], MD, Director and Founder of the Institute for Integrative Psychiatry in New York, has more than 25 years' experience working with divorcing women. Dr. Kaminski told me that the emotional reactions to divorce fall generally into two groups.

Obviously your emotional reactions would depend on who initiated the divorce, the circumstances, whether there are young children and the respective personalities involved in the process," he said. "But in general, there are two main 'groups of feelings': 1) feelings towards your soon to become ex, and 2) feelings you experience towards yourself."

It might not surprise you to learn that your feelings about your husband can seem like a virtual stew of anger, hurt, disbelief, deep sadness, rage, and shame, but can also reach heights of profound relief, and a sense of liberation and adventure. Dr. Kaminski said that this wide range of emotion is very common to women going through a divorce.

"You may find yourself going through the entire gamut several times a day, or maddeningly feeling all of them together," he added. "That is normal and a common part of almost every divorce process."

It's likely that the more complicated group of emotions you're experiencing centers on your feelings about yourself. "Those feelings are complicated and nuanced rather than intense; particular to you rather than universal; much less clear and poorly defined," Dr. Kaminski explained. "However, the way you feel towards yourself during and after the divorce, is a determining factor regarding your personal recovery. Even more so, your inner dialogue determines your ability to forge a trusting relationship with a future person. Indeed, one of the issues that haunts women in divorce is the sense that they had made a mistake in choosing their mate: left unaddressed it can lead to a loss of confidence in their ability to make future choices."

Clearly, you'll have a tremendous amount to cope with as you divorce. Don't go it alone.

I learned more about the importance of self care to a healthy emotional state from Kristin Davin[3], Psy.D., a licensed clinical psychologist in New York City. Dr. Davin has been in practice for more than 10 years, helping both men and women transition through the challenges of divorce.

"It is important to remain healthy and take care of yourself during this very emotional and physically challenging process," she said. "People often forget to take care of themselves and often many of the healthy habits they had prior to the divorce, quickly go by the wayside due to stress, anxiety, depression, and feeling simply overwhelmed by the process. This is a key time to do what you can to take care of yourself."

During your divorce, you should keep making healthy choices about exercise, food, and decompression time. Structuring your days can help keep you on track. "Too much unstructured time equals negative thoughts, more anxiety, and sadness," she advised. "Be in the moment. Accept your feelings as they arise. Journaling helps."

Davin also cautioned against letting yourself become isolated from family and friends. "That supportive network is invaluable," she said.

While you'll definitely rely on loved ones to buoy your spirits, there is good reason to have a professional therapist on your team.

How do you find a therapist?

First, you'll need to decide whether you need a psychiatrist (a medical doctor who can prescribe drugs), a psychologist, or another licensed practitioner. If you have medical needs (for an antidepressant, anti-anxiety medicine, sleeping aid, etc.) be sure you see a psychiatrist.

Once you have an idea what kind of professional will best meet your needs, check out online resources such as Psychology Today[4], Network Therapy[5], and Good Therapy[6].

"These websites offer a profile on each therapist (master's level, doctoral level) and provide valuable information," Davin said. "You can do a 'search' according to area, zip code, or key terms such as divorce therapist or divorce or separation."

Narrowing the search often involves a short interview, either in-person or on the phone.

"I think the most important question to ask a therapist is about their experience. Do they have experience? How much? What is their style of treatment when helping people go through a divorce?" Davin said. "Aside from having experience, importance is placed on the therapeutic alliance, the relationship that is created between the therapist and the patient. Do not be afraid to interview more than one therapist. It is about the 'fit.' If you feel comfortable with the therapist, then therapy is often beneficial on many levels. Much good work can occur when this relationship has been established."

If you find after a while that the professional relationship isn't working, you should speak up and make a change, if necessary.

"If you feel stuck, or unrelated, you should not hesitate to bring it up with the therapist, and if nothing changes, seek another one," Dr. Kaminski suggested. "Most of us can tell, instinctively, whether the psychiatrist we work with is helpful or not. Ultimately, the feeling of being genuinely helped is the crucial criterion in treatment."

That feeling of being "genuinely helped" is not something you can achieve on your own. Please abandon any notion that you should just tough it out, emotionally, during your divorce. Aside from the many benefits to your well-being, getting expert help with the emotional roller coaster of divorce means you'll be thinking much more clearly when it comes to the important financial decisions you have before you. You've got an attorney to handle the legal aspects of your case, and a divorce financial advisor to look after the financial details. For your emotional needs, you need a qualified, compassionate therapist on your professional divorce team[7] as well.

Reminder: You can expect divorce to be an emotional roller coaster. Remind yourself often that in time, it will get better. "This, too, shall pass."

Hot tip: In searching for a therapist, your divorce attorney might also be a great source of professional contacts. Recommendations from friends and family can also be invaluable. Keep in mind, though, that a therapist that's working wonders for your best friend, or who testified beautifully at your attorney's last trial, may just not work for you—and don't be afraid to say so, if that's the case.

Legal matters: Especially when child custody is an issue during a divorce, expert psychiatric testimony is sometimes required. However, many mental health professionals are reluctant to testify in court. When you're interviewing prospective therapists, find out early on whether s/he is willing and able to do so. Make sure you choose a person whose professional demeanor will serve you well.

CHAPTER 10

WHEN TO CALL IN A REAL ESTATE APPRAISER

Negotiating a divorce property settlement depends on a fair, impartial, and accurate assessment of the value of all marital property. But, how do you determine how much the real estate portion of your portfolio is worth? You certainly should *not* rely on your husband's opinion or a neighbor's "guesstimate." The value of real estate isn't even something a mediator or a judge can decide.

When it's time for an accurate evaluation of the value of real estate property, you'll need the expertise of a professional real estate appraiser. Here's why:

A real estate appraiser's job is to determine the fair market value of your property, and in most cases, that determination is made by comparing your property to recent, similar sales in the area.

Don't make the mistake of thinking the value of your property is related to what you paid when you purchased it. Real estate markets are fluid, and the value of your real estate depends on what market conditions are like *today.*

To determine fair market value, an appraiser will inspect your property, making special note of any unique features. Then, he/she will identify comparable properties that have recently sold in the same market. Keep in mind: The more recent sales there are to compare to, the more confident you can be that these sale prices reflect actual market conditions. (If there's one particularly low or high price, it's an outlier that's not representative of a typical sale for the area.) The comparable sales, in conjunction with any special features of your property, are used to determine a number that represents the appraiser's best assessment of fair market value for your property.

Part of the real estate appraiser's expertise is in knowing how different real estate amenities contribute (or not) to market value—and that's why it's essential your property is appraised by a dispassionate professional.

Homeowners are often disappointed to find that the costly improvements they're quite proud of are actually much less valuable to potential buyers than they'd expected. Some features, such as swimming pools, can actually add less to the market value of a property than what it cost to install them! The appraiser's report will be rendered without bias or emotional attachment to the window treatments, the cabana lighting or that peaceful Zen garden you adore.

Real estate appraisers have expertise in the local real estate markets where they work.

If your financial portfolio includes real estate in different markets, it is very important to engage appraisers who are familiar with those markets. Why? Because fair market value for a condo in Aspen, Colorado isn't best evaluated by an expert on the real estate market in Westchester County, New York. Similarly, fair market values in locations with a large proportion of second homes, be it Nantucket or Naples, Palm Beach, or Palm Springs, are most accurately assessed by professionals who work in those markets. Make sure you hire an appraiser who has expert knowledge of the market in which you'll be selling.

Real estate values change over time.

Even though most real estate appraisals focus on fair market value *today*, some divorcing women may need to call on a real estate appraiser to determine what a property was worth at some time in the past. This is called an historical, or "retrospective", appraisal.

For example, if you married your husband and moved into a home he already owned, there was likely no appraisal of its value at that time. However, as part of your divorce settlement process—and dependent on the division of property regulations in your state[1]—you might want to show that the property has gained value[2] over your marriage, perhaps due to improvements you made to it with marital funds. You'll need good estimates of its fair market value then and now. On the other side of that coin, a retrospective appraisal is also worth having if you sell a property at a loss and need to determine how much of that loss was incurred during the marriage.

Divorce appraisals are becoming more and more common.

According to an article in *The Wall Street Journal*[3], appraisals required for divorce proceedings represent an increasing proportion of real estate appraisers' business, and due to their potentially litigious context, a divorce appraisal may cost several times as much as a simple appraisal for a real estate transaction or refinance.

Clearly, real estate appraisals can play a pivotal role in your divorce settlement agreement, but also keep these two fundamental factors in mind:

1. **Fair market value is only part of the story.** Once you have determined the fair market value, you'll need to subtract the existing mortgages to find out what your current equity is in the property.

2. **Your equity in the property is not the same as money in the bank!**

If you can sell your property for more than you paid, you may owe both Federal and state capital gains tax after your $250,000 exclusion as a single woman. (Two important notes: 1) This $250K exclusion is applicable only to your primary residence, not your vacation or investment real estate, 2) Federal capital gains taxes were raised in 2013 and can now range from 15 to 23.8 percent.)

Here's a simple example to illustrate my point. Let's say the appraised fair market value of your house is $1,000,000. You have a $400,000 mortgage and you originally paid $200,000 for the house. Your selling costs are 6 percent or $60,000.

The $1,000,000 sales price minus $60,000 selling costs = $940,000.

Since your original purchase price was $200,000, $940,000 - $200,000 = $740,000 profit.

$740,000 profit - $250,000 exclusion on primary residence = $490,000 capital gains.

For simplicity, let's assume your total capital gains tax rate is 20 percent. $490,000 capital gains X 20 percent = $98,000 capital gains tax due.

So . . . What do you end up with after the sale? $940,000 after selling costs minus outstanding $400,000 mortgage minus $98,000 capital gains tax = $442,000

That $442,000 is now somewhat comparable to $442,000 in the bank. Why do I say only "somewhat comparable?" Because until you sell it, your real estate has carrying costs that money in the bank doesn't have—real estate taxes, mortgage payments, water and sewerage bills, landscaping, fuel, repairs, maintenance, etc.

Reminder: Negotiating a fair divorce property settlement is complicated . . . and it can be difficult. You want your settlement to be determined based on true, accurate and complete information, and as always, the best possible outcome depends on having experts on your team[4] who can anticipate the subtleties of the settlement process. Whether you and your spouse own one primary residence or many properties spread far and wide, a qualified real estate appraiser has a critical role to play in this process.

Hot tip: The property's value as assessed by municipal authorities for tax purposes is also researched as part of the appraisal process, but it isn't directly related to fair market value. Your property appraisal may come in much higher or lower than the assessed value used to calculate your property tax bill.

Legal matters: For many residential properties, an appraisal is fairly easy to substantiate or defend. But what if you own the only property in the area with a deep water dock, a greenhouse, a stable, or a four-car garage? Because unique features like these may be evaluated differently by different appraisers, appraisers' conclusions can vary, sometimes considerably. When there is a substantial difference between each side's appraisal of a property, a judge may require that a third independent appraisal be conducted.

CHAPTER 11

THE VOCATIONAL EXPERT: AN IMPORTANT MEMBER OF YOUR DIVORCE TEAM

If you're beginning to research the divorce process, or even just thinking about it, you have probably already realized that the days of simply hiring a good divorce lawyer and letting him/her handle everything are long, long gone. Today's divorces can be exceedingly complicated, and many spheres of professional expertise typically come into play.

For example, many divorcing women now find they need to enlist the professional services of a vocational expert, someone whose job it is to know what skills are in demand in today's employment market and what income those skills can command in various careers.

What does a vocational expert do?

A vocational expert meets with a client in one or more sessions to assess the client's abilities, interests, education, experience, and other qualifications. These are then examined against the backdrop of the current employment market where the client lives or is planning to relocate.

Based on this analysis, the vocational expert evaluates the likelihood that the client can get a job and estimates what the client can expect to earn. Earnings projections can be made for both short- and long-term consideration.

The vocational expert's recommendations can be provided solely for the client's personal use, or if required as part of a legal proceeding, they can be included in a formal report to the court.

What does that have to do with your divorce?

Well, a major part of your settlement negotiation process will be to evaluate how much spousal and/ or child support will have to be paid, and by whom. A vocational expert's evaluation of you and/or your husband could be required by the court, or presented voluntarily, for consideration in determining what those payments should be.

Here are four reasons to have a vocational expert in your corner during divorce:

» ***To obtain an objective, professional assessment of your spouse's earning potential.***
Some high-grossing husbands try to get their

alimony and/or child support obligations calculated based on a much lower income than they actually earn. Your husband may claim that his earnings have suddenly tanked due to poor economic conditions. He may even quit his job or take a lower-paying position during the divorce, only so that his alimony and child support payments will be less. These are underhanded tactics, and they're particularly difficult to understand when child support is involved.

A vocational expert can help cut through devious strategies and false assertions and get to the facts of the matter: What can your husband reasonably be expected to earn? If his income has legitimately decreased, how much is it likely to rebound, and how soon?

» ***To get a realistic idea of your own employability and earning potential.***
Especially if you have advanced degrees or special training, your husband may claim that you're fully capable of earning a six-figure income, even if you've been entirely out of the workforce for many years. This is probably completely unrealistic, but how will you prove it?

If, like many women, you gave up paid work to care for your children, you'll want to know what your current employment prospects truly are, and what you can expect to earn if you re-enter the workforce. A vocational expert can tell you how your education and work history position you in today's job market, and whether you'll need additional training to update your skills.

» ***To provide a second opinion if your spouse has hired a vocational expert, or if a vocational evaluation is court-ordered.***
If you are requesting alimony as part of your divorce settlement, your husband can request that a vocational evaluation be conducted to determine how much you could earn in the current job market. Your projected earning potential is then imputed, or assigned a value, and the alimony your husband will be required to pay could be reduced by that amount. For example, if you are well-qualified to work in a field where available jobs pay $50,000/year, but you choose instead to take a job in an antique shop and earn $20,000, it is possible your husband's spousal support obligation would be calculated based on the $50,000 you "could" be earning.

So, you see, there can be a significant amount at stake. Providing the court with a second vocational consultant's report is a good move. If your own vocational expert's conclusions agree with those from your husband's expert, so be it. If they differ dramatically, then it is more likely that the court will make a determination somewhere in the middle than just accept one report over the other without question. Either way, you're better off hiring your own vocational expert.

» *To evaluate and document changes in employability or earning capacity.*
The assessments performed by a vocational expert can objectively document changes in your ability to earn. For example, you may someday experience an illness or injury that prevents you from working as you once did, or earning what you once could. If this has happened to you during your marriage, you may need to prove that your earning potential is no longer what it was when you were first married. I can assure you that your husband is not likely to bring it up on his own.

In any case, a vocational expert can provide the court with an objective description of your limitations so that spousal support can be appropriately calculated or adjusted right away, and also help you find fulfilling work that's possible for you to do in the long term.

You may also need a vocational consultant's expertise if you believe your spouse's circumstances have changed such that an adjustment in his alimony and/or child support payments to you is warranted. A vocational expert can corroborate that opinion for the court.

The array of specialized services and expertise available for couples going through divorce today is extraordinary. You won't necessarily need to hire a professional to weigh in on every single aspect of your divorce, but it's important to know what help is available. Vocational experts play a unique and important role in divorce settlement negotiations, and the advantages of consulting with one can long outlast the divorce process.

Reminder: To determine spousal support (also called alimony or maintenance) and/or child support, assumptions are often made about your husband's earning potential, and about yours. Make sure you have a voice in this process! Vocational expertise can help ensure these assumptions are reasonable and fair.

Hot tip: Quite apart from their use in your divorce, results of interest and aptitude tests from the vocational evaluation process can be truly valuable for your future personal and professional growth. Think of the evaluation as an opportunity to invest in yourself, and get as much out of it as you can. You may even find you want to revisit the vocational consultant in the future, for guidance in making a career change or even in launching your own business.

Legal matters: In some states, a vocational evaluation is mandatory whenever alimony is requested as part of a divorce settlement. If you are required to cooperate with a vocational evaluation, whether it is requested by your spouse or by state law, it is in your best interest to have your own expert conduct one as well, so that both sides are fairly represented to the court.

CHAPTER 12

CHANGING THESE TWO PERSPECTIVES CAN HELP YOU PREPARE FOR DIVORCE

M y goal is to help women come through their divorces in optimum financial shape, with settlements that last as long as possible, and my advice early in the divorce process focuses on mental preparedness, as well as on the nuts and bolts of financial preparedness. I urge you to learn about divorce laws where you live, develop a good understanding of what you're about to face, become thoroughly familiar with your marital financial situation and most importantly, to *Think Financially, Not Emotionally*®[1], come what may.

But here's the problem: Over the years, I've come to recognize that there are two prevailing attitudes that may significantly interfere with your ability to prepare for divorce in the ways I'm suggesting. These societal mindsets, while evolving, still hold sway with a surprising number of divorcing women. They are:

1. that being divorced somehow brands a woman as defective or inferior, and
2. that in marriage, husbands are better suited to handling the finances than are wives.

Let's explore each one of these in more detail.

In the past, divorce was considered scandalous and immoral—something to be discussed in hushed tones—and many divorced women found themselves effectively shunned. Today, because it's so much more common than it used to be, divorce no longer carries that kind of social stigma. Even if not divorced ourselves, we all have friends or family who've been through it. Who's left to do the stigmatizing?

Of course, I'm not implying that as a divorced woman you'll *never* face an awkward moment. Social norms can take a very long time to neutralize or reverse, and I still see areas where our cultural mindset needs to progress even further toward acceptance. When we all begin to treat divorce not as a travesty, but simply as something that some couples undergo, women won't feel that isolation any longer.

The second societal mindset—that husbands are better than wives at financial matters—is the one that worries me more. All too often, even among younger couples, it's still common for men to handle investments, insurance, taxes, retirement savings, major purchases, etc., while women control the day-to-day spending and leave those more consequential issues to their husbands. It is my strong opinion that this arrangement is harmful to women, and it is time to make it a thing of the past.

I'll be blunt: There should be nothing about your marital finances that you aren't familiar with and to which you don't have complete, unfettered access. If it takes some educational catching up to become familiar with all aspects of your financial portfolio, then so be it. Get yourself informed. There are excellent resources available for financial education at every level.

From your earliest days together, you and your husband should be absolute equals when it comes to making financial decisions. It doesn't matter if your incomes are not equal; few couples are in that situation. What matters is that you have regular, sit-down discussions of your finances and long-term goals, and that your thoughts, opinions and questions are given equal weight in those discussions. I often suggest that couples do this quarterly, to coincide with the issuance of investment earnings statements. Whatever interval makes financial and practical sense to you both, honor the commitment and stick to it.

Frequent, open and clear communication about finances is excellent for marriages, as it alleviates many common troubles that worsen over time.

Once you fully reject the negative and damaging notions that divorce is shameful and that men are better with money, you'll find that preparedness for divorce comes much more easily. You'll be more confident that you can handle what divorce will bring. You'll understand that it's crucial to prepare for a financially secure future[2] as a single woman, and you'll take an active role in forging that future.

Being in that active, empowered role means taking the four concrete steps to financial preparedness that I've written about in Volume I and then, even more extensively in the pages that follow in Volume II. You need to:

1. Get your financial paperwork in order[3].
2. Assess your credit and open your own bank accounts.
3. Set aside enough money to fund your divorce.
4. Line up your professional divorce team[4].

Ending a marriage isn't easy, but neither is it shameful. Hold your head high, get the financial savvy you need, and face your divorce from a position of confidence and strength.

Reminder: If you're going through a divorce and catch yourself feeling defective or in any way "less than," think about these famous words of Eleanor Roosevelt: "Nobody can make you feel inferior without your consent."

Hot tip: If you *Think Financially, Not Emotionally*[®5] during your divorce, that can save you from financial disaster, but it doesn't mean that your emotions aren't real or important. Have a therapist on your divorce team to keep you in good emotional health, so that your focus can be on financial matters when it's most needed.

Legal matters: If your attorney ever belittles, side-steps or refuses to answer your questions, call him/her out on it. You should never get a "don't worry your pretty little head about that" vibe from any divorce professional. Anyone who doesn't treat your questions with respect is not a good fit for your team.

DIVIDING ASSETS & DEBTS

Do you have questions about "the basics" of dividing assets and debts in divorce? In Volume I, I reviewed why it's important to know if you live in an Equitable Distribution State or a Community Property State, the difference between marital property and separate property, and the definitions of key terms such as Date of Separation, Valuation Date, active appreciation, etc. Here, in Volume II, I'll tackle specifics regarding Financial Affidavits, why you need a Lifestyle Analysis, how to deal with difficult-to-divide assets such as art, how to divide stocks, restricted stock and stock options, and what you need to know about inheritances and gifts, pets, and student loans/college tuition.

CHAPTER 13

ANSWER THESE FIVE QUESTIONS BEFORE FILING YOUR FINANCIAL AFFIDAVIT

In all contested divorces—and even in some un-contested ones—the courts require each spouse to file what's called a "Financial Affidavit," a formal document that details the factors that typically play a role in the finances of every marriage: how much you earn (income), how much you spend (expenses), how much you own (assets), how much you owe (liabilities/debt), etc.

If you're asked to complete one, your Financial Affidavit will provide the court with a snapshot, so to speak, of your current financial picture. What's more, it compels both you and your husband to swear you are telling the truth about your finances.

Now at first, I'm sure the idea of a Financial Affidavit sounds relatively simple. All you need to do is get the questionnaire-type form and start filling in the answers, right? Well, unfortunately, it's not quite so easy.

You see, determining accurate figures for income, expenses, assets, and liabilities can become rather complex—especially if you haven't been an active participant in your family finances in the past. And complicating matters even more is the fact that this document essentially creates the foundation for your future financial well-being. How? Because the courts use Financial Affidavits when deciding alimony, child support (including temporary alimony and support), and the division of property.

Therefore, it's absolutely critical that the numbers you include are completely accurate. Here are five key questions to answer to help ensure you give your Financial Affidavit the thoughtful, careful attention it deserves:

Do you have the form that's required in your state? As with many aspects of divorce, such as the division of separate and marital property, the division of debt, etc., the regulations governing Financial Affidavits differ depending on where you live. To start with, Financial Affidavits are called different things in different states. In New Jersey, divorcing couples file a "Case Information Statement." Meanwhile, the courts in Utah require a "Financial Declaration," and in Connecticut, it's simply called a Financial Affidavit. In New York, we use a "Statement of Net Worth."

Are you "guess-timating?" I hope not! Remember: When it comes to Financial Affidavits, even the "little" details can make a "big" difference. You may cringe at the prospect of sorting through the past few years of assorted credit card bills, utility payments, bank statements, etc. But, knowing your finances at that level of detail can make a significant difference in the financial picture you present to the court. No matter how difficult the process becomes, resist the urge to guesstimate! Most people guess wrong—and usually, they're *wildly* wrong.

How carefully will your divorce attorney review your work? Although your divorce attorney will provide you with the proper forms and fundamental guidance, don't expect them to use a fine-tooth comb to go through the numbers you submit. At best, most divorce attorneys will check for only the most glaring mistakes, and quite honestly, they really don't have the time or inclination to verify your mortgage bills, canceled checks, etc. or sort through several years of your credit card statements to determine what each and every charge was for (clothing, groceries, restaurant, gas, gifts, etc.). In other words, if you show your monthly telephone expense at $5,000 or you're spending 30% of your monthly income on clothing, they'll question you. But don't expect them to know if you've forgotten to include the garage costs for your car or if you're really spending $1,000 per month on clothing not $100 (unless that amount sticks out as a very large percentage of your income or expenses).

Are you prepared to swear the information you're providing is true? When you file your Financial Affidavit you must swear under oath (usually before a notary public) that the information you provided is true and correct to the best of your knowledge and belief. Obviously, your husband will have to do the same when he files his Financial Affidavit. That means he can't "accidentally" overlook telling you about the vacation he just charged on your jointly-held credit card or the raise he got three months ago. Anyone who intentionally provides false information on a Financial Affidavit is committing perjury and could face serious legal action. (That's not to say it doesn't happen. Unfortunately, your husband *may* lie on his Financial Affidavit, and if he's caught, he could face severe consequences, including forfeiture of the assets he lied about).

Are you feeling stressed? If you feel overwhelmed by the task of completing your Financial Affidavit, consult with a divorce financial advisor[1] who can complete both the Financial Affidavit and a Lifestyle Analysis on your behalf. As I'll discuss in the next chapter, a Lifestyle Analysis identifies the spending habits of a couple along with the day-to-day living expenses incurred during their marriage, with an emphasis on the last three to five years. It includes recurring and ordinary expenses, as well as unusual and non-recurring expenses. It's often required by the judge and serves as a verification of the net worth and income and expense statements submitted by both spouses.

Reminder: The information you include on your Financial Affidavit will be used to determine the division of your assets, alimony, and even child support. So, omissions and/or errors in this document could have a significant impact on the financial outcome of your divorce. Please make certain you prepare your Financial Affidavit properly. In most cases, it creates the foundation for your future financial well-being.

Hot tip: Your Financial Affidavit can be revised. If your financial circumstances change, you can—and should—update your Financial Affidavit (even after it's filed with the courts).

Legal matters: Sometimes, during the process of completing your Financial Affidavit and/or Lifestyle Analysis, you may discover that your husband is hiding assets. (This happens much more often than most women realize.) Since anyone who prepares a Financial Affidavit must swear under oath that the figures provided are true, your husband can be held in contempt of court and can face additional sanctions, including possible criminal charges, if he submits false information.

CHAPTER 14

WHY YOU NEED A LIFESTYLE ANALYSIS

A carefully-researched, comprehensive Lifestyle Analysis could very well make the difference between a financially successful divorce settlement agreement and one that is considerably less favorable. So, why don't more divorcing women have a Lifestyle Analysis prepared? My hunch is that many women (and their attorneys) simply don't understand how valuable this level of financial inquiry can be to their financial future.

Don't let yourself be one of these uninformed women! Instead, let's have a discussion that starts at the beginning, with the answer to this basic—but extremely relevant—question:

What Is a Lifestyle Analysis?

In essence, a Lifestyle Analysis establishes what your standard of living was during the marriage. It reconstructs:

1. the day-to-day living expenses incurred during your marriage and
2. the spending habits of both you and your husband.

Generally, a Lifestyle Analysis has an emphasis on the last several years of your marriage, and it usually includes, but is not limited to, an analysis of:

» all financial statements (bank, brokerage, credit cards, etc.)
» personal and business income tax returns
» recurring and ordinary expenses within each category of expense (clothing, food, housing, entertainment, travel, etc.)
» unusual, non-recurring and/or seasonal expenses
» Any discrepancies
» credit reports

Now at first, compiling the data needed for a Lifestyle Analysis might seem daunting—especially because it demands your time at the beginning of the divorce process, which is when you may be feeling the most stressed. However, the process of preparing a Lifestyle Analysis truly *does* deserve your attention. Here's why:

Your Financial Affidavit may not be accurate. If you've already begun the divorce process, it's likely your attorney has asked you to complete a form commonly referred to as a "Financial Affidavit." As I discussed in the previous chapter, this form details your income, expenses, assets, and liabilities, and so, it gives the court a "snapshot," so to speak, of your current financial picture. The courts use the information included in the Financial Affidavit to decide fundamental financial matters about your case, including alimony, child support (both temporary alimony and support), and the division of property.

In a nutshell, your Financial Affidavit lays the groundwork for your financial future. But, will anyone make sure you've completed it correctly? Will anyone check over your calculations to verify they're accurate and/or remind you if you've forgotten anything? Probably not. Your divorce attorney certainly won't comb through all your tax returns, bank account, brokerage account, and credit card statements to confirm your results. Instead, absent any glaring errors, your attorney will typically rely on the information you provided, and he/she will assume that it is correct. (In fact, you will have to sign a statement on the forms attesting, under penalty of perjury, that the information you provided is correct.)

"Little" mistakes or omissions on your Financial Affidavit can have "big" consequences. Because most women (and their husbands for that matter) don't know how to accurately complete a Financial Affidavit, they often miscalculate the values needed. Others resort to "guess-timating," because they don't have access to the information they need, or because they don't know how to find and/or compute it, or because the process just seems too difficult/time-consuming and most people think it's okay to fluff it off—not realizing how important those numbers are to their case and their future financial security.

You see, estimating or guessing when filling out Financial Affidavits can prove disastrous. Do you really want alimony determined based on what you "think" your monthly mortgage payments are? A carefully prepared Lifestyle Analysis will shine a spotlight on any errors or omissions and help ensure your Financial Affidavit is as accurate as possible.

A Lifestyle Analysis may be required by the courts. In many divorces, the courts use the details in a Lifestyle Analysis to verify the net worth and income and expense statements submitted by both spouses. In short, it can help a judge determine the amount of your divorce financial judgment including the amount and duration of alimony.

A Lifestyle Analysis may uncover hidden assets . . . and perhaps even a husband's dirty tricks. Any comprehensive investigation of spending habits and day-to-day living expenses is bound to reveal a few surprises here or there. However, in some cases, the details uncovered by a Lifestyle Analysis can be even more shocking. In fact, sometimes, when we are preparing a Lifestyle Analysis for a client, we find non-recurring or occasional expenses that take her totally by surprise. You see, unfortunately, it's not unusual during this process to discover a husband has been pursuing some kind of nefarious activity, such as selling marital assets, concealing income, collecting art, or even supporting an extramarital relationship completely unbeknownst to his wife.

Once revealed through the analysis, this dissipation of assets can be taken into consideration when the judge determines the amount of your divorce settlement and any alimony ordered.

A Lifestyle Analysis can form the basis for a post-divorce budget. Once the Lifestyle Analysis is completed, you'll have a more accurate picture of what funds are required to maintain your standard of living. The analysis will help determine how much you and your husband spent on an average basis month-to-month and year-to-year, and you can use these calculations as a guide to help you develop a budget for yourself as a single woman/mother.

Who should prepare my Lifestyle Analysis?

In some cases, your divorce attorney or his/her paralegal may offer to assist you with a Lifestyle Analysis or another financial aspect of your divorce, but he or she is unlikely to have the specialized training and expertise in divorce finances to do so as thoroughly, efficiently, or cost-effectively as a divorce financial advisor will. Even CPAs and financial advisors are unlikely to realize what analyses and projections they ought to conduct on your behalf. It's not that these professionals aren't competent at what they do; it's just that divorce finance is simply not their specialty, so they haven't had the advanced training or hands-on experience needed.

For example, while CPAs can provide good historical and present-day financial snapshots, few carry out future projections—and yet it's these future projections that will show you whether your future is likely to be financially secure or not based on various divorce settlement options/proposals.

Similarly, only a scant 1 percent of financial advisors have earned the Certified Divorce Financial Analyst™ designation, and most of them have not completed additional training or education in the field of divorce finance and law. In fact, many large financial services firms, including Merrill Lynch, Morgan Stanley, UBS, and Wells Fargo, typically don't permit their financial advisors to provide advice on real estate or closely held businesses, and yet for many couples, these represent the vast majority of their net worth.

 Reminder: The early stages of divorce can be emotionally trying and confusing on many levels, and during that time, compiling the data needed for a Lifestyle Analysis might seem like an overwhelming, time-consuming chore. It may even seem like the last thing you want to concern yourself with as you start navigating the rocky waters of divorce. However, you need to remember that the end result is extremely valuable. Ultimately, your goal is to receive the most equitable distribution of assets possible, and a Lifestyle Analysis provides the basis for credible arguments that can demonstrate the cost of supporting the lifestyle you are accustomed to.

Hot tip: Divorce attorneys welcome the expertise and support of a qualified divorce financial advisor when it comes to the daunting task of conducting a Lifestyle Analysis or providing complex financial projections that justify their client's position at the negotiating table or in court.

Legal matters: The rules, regulations and terminology governing divorce can vary from state to state. So, the form that's commonly known as a "Financial Affidavit" may be called something different where you live. For example, in New York, a form like this is called a Statement of Net Worth. In New Jersey, it's known as a Case Information Statement. The courts in Utah call it a Financial Declaration.

CHAPTER 15

PLEASE, DON'T TAKE YOUR HUSBAND'S WORD ABOUT WHO GETS WHAT

I have worked with many women over the years who, at our initial consultation, admit to having no idea of exactly how much they own or owe. "I know we're doing fine, but my husband handles all the particulars," they tell me.

I promise, I'm not here to berate you if this has been your situation. While I always advise brides[1] to be full and equal partners in marital financial matters, I understand that even today, in many marriages, finances are the sole realm of the husband.

However, if your marriage is ending in divorce, I *am* here to tell you that it's time to do some catching up on the financial front. Knowledge is power, and in divorce, you need both.

Yes, your attorney can handle the legal issues, and yes, your divorce financial advisor will absolutely work with you to determine the strategies that will result in the best possible outcome for your financial future. But as the most important member of your divorce team, it is important that YOU know where you stand, and how your marital assets and debts will be divided.

It's not likely that your husband will encourage you to become well-informed. On the contrary, husbands who've had total control of finances in the marriage will, when divorce is in the works, often try to lead their wives to believe that they won't be entitled to certain assets.

For example, he will be all too happy to have you believe you're not entitled to any of his 401(k) because it is "part of his job, and you had nothing to do with it." He'll be delighted to keep you under the erroneous impression that his stock options can't be divided in the divorce because they come solely from his association with the company and/or he hasn't exercised them yet. And he will be in no hurry to correct you if you think you aren't entitled to part of the value of physical assets such as houses, cars, and boats, because his is the only name on the title.

How do you guard against this misinformation?

The first step is to become familiar with the difference between separate property and marital property[2]. Granted, some states, such as Connecticut, Massachusetts, Michigan, and Vermont, do not typically distinguish between marital and separate property, but most states do—even if what the law considers separate property is actually pretty limited. For example, in most states, separate property is restricted to:

» Property that was owned by either spouse prior to the marriage or after the Date of Separation.
» An inheritance received by either spouse, either before or after the marriage, if not commingled or merged with marital assets.
» A gift either spouse receives from a third party (i.e., the pearls your grandmother gave you).
» Monies received as the "pain and suffering" part of a personal injury judgment (again, if not mingled with marital assets, as in a joint bank account).
» Property designated as separate as per a prenuptial or postnuptial agreement.

Everything else you and your husband have acquired during the marriage is usually considered marital property, regardless of "ownership" or title.

That includes the 401(k), the stock options, and the boat he keeps in Florida that you've never even seen. (Aha—had you forgotten about the boat? Just because you never enjoyed deep-sea fishing doesn't mean you aren't entitled to some of its value, if it was bought with marital funds while you were married.)

What other marital assets might there be, that until recently you had no reason to consider? Especially if you haven't been paying particularly close attention before, now's the time to do some serious thinking about what you and your husband have accumulated over the years of your marriage. Your divorce financial advisor can help.

As you work through your divorce settlement negotiations, don't assume there is anything you absolutely don't have a right to. Now that you're divorcing, your best financial interest and your soon-to-be-ex-husband's are likely in direct opposition. You should never take his word for it when he says you have no claim on certain assets.

Reminder: As convincing a person as your husband might be, you must *Think Financially, Not Emotionally*®³ when considering what he tells you. Even better, say a firm "thanks, but no thanks" to his opinion, and enlist expert help of your own.

Hot tip: Does your husband continually dodge certain questions? Is there something he seems especially keen on steering your attention away from? Don't let these things slide. Even though it's illegal, many husbands try to hide marital assets⁴ to keep them out of divorce settlement negotiations. The more informed you are, the more easily you'll be able to pick up on the telltale signs that your husband may be hiding marital assets during your divorce[5]. (See Volume I, Chapter 20 for more details.)

Legal matters: You should consult with your divorce attorney about division of marital assets. Laws and definitions vary from state to state. If you will be the one to file, and you have homes in more than one state and a choice of jurisdictions, it is worth consulting with legal experts in each to help you decide.

CHAPTER 16

WHAT DIVORCING WOMEN NEED TO KNOW ABOUT DIVIDING STOCK

Divorce has many different dimensions (emotional, social, physical, etc.), but *financially speaking*, it all boils down to the division of assets and debts. Of the many kinds of assets that are divided by divorcing couples, stocks represent some of the most anxiety-inducing. Why? Because stocks are important and valuable—and they can also be risky and uncertain. Many people don't know quite how to handle stock market investments and have a general uneasiness that they're not doing the right thing. At best, they're worried they're not maximizing their benefits; at worst, they fear they could be risking financial disaster.

While I'm not here to discuss the relative advantages of small- and large-cap stocks, or whether it's a good time to invest in biotechnology or agribusiness,

I *can* help with some of the uncertainty you're likely to be feeling about how stocks are divided in divorce.

Here are a few general steps to help you better understand your stock portfolio:

Inventory what you own and determine whether it is separate or marital property[1].

Some of your assets will be considered separate property; others will be considered marital property. (See the previous chapter for a detailed discussion about the differences between the two.)

Please note that stocks acquired prior to your marriage will usually be considered separate property only *if they have not been commingled with marital assets.* If you had stock given to you before you wed—as a graduation present, for example—it would qualify as separate property unless you later merged those shares with holdings you and your husband own together, or added to it with additional shares purchased with marital funds. (In some states, if you actively manage your portfolio, any increase in value of that separate property might be considered marital property. For more information on active appreciation, see Volume I, Chapter 12.)

Understand that how your marital property will be divided depends on where you live.

Do you live in a "Community Property" State, or an "Equitable Distribution State?"[2] In a **Community Property State,** each spouse is typically considered to be an equal owner of all marital property, and upon divorce, the division is 50-50.

Arizona, California, Idaho, Louisiana, Nevada, New Mexico, Texas, Washington, and Wisconsin are Community Property States. Alaskans can "opt in" for community property, and Puerto Rico is a community property jurisdiction.

The other 41 states are **equitable distribution, or "common law," states**. In an Equitable Distribution State, the person whose name appears on an asset (e.g. the deed to a house, title to a car, or stock), is considered the owner, but in a divorce, each spouse has the legal right to claim a fair and equitable portion of those assets.

"Fair and equitable" does not necessarily mean a 50-50 split. The goal in an Equitable Distribution State is not that each spouse gets half the marital assets, but that a fair division be made based on careful, complete consideration of each spouse's circumstances.

Now, let's discuss some considerations specific to dividing stock portfolios.

Know the difference between the cost basis of your stock holdings and their current value. Your future tax exposure depends on it.

The *cost basis* of stock is the price you originally paid for it. It's very important to know, because capital gains tax is based on the investment's appreciation— that is, the difference between what you paid, and what you sold it for.

[135]

So let's say you and your husband have an investment portfolio worth $200K. Seems fair to agree to a 50-50 split, so you'd each get $100K, right?

Not so fast! With stocks, it's more complicated than that. Pay close attention to which specific holdings would be in your half. If your husband is savvy, he may want his half to only include stocks, mutual funds, etc. with values close to their cost basis. In return, he'll happily let you have $100K worth of investments that have appreciated in value, leaving you with the burden of huge capital gains taxes to pay on those appreciated shares when you sell them!

How huge? Assume, for the sake of discussion, that the cost basis of the shares he now wants you to keep is $40K. That means your $100K portfolio represents an appreciation of $60K. Depending on your income, the federal capital gains tax in 2014 is currently as much as 23.8 percent! Even assuming you don't qualify for the 3.8% surtax, and pay "only" 20 percent tax on your $60K capital gain, that is $12K you'll have to shell out that your husband will not.

So, if you stick with his suggestion, you *won't* end up with $100K. You'll only get $88K (and that's before subtracting the additional capital gains taxes that some states impose).

The same capital gains tax scenario does not apply to 401(k)s, IRAs and other retirement funds, because capital gains on investments within those retirement vehicles are tax-deferred. You will pay ordinary income taxes when you withdraw funds (no penalty if you are older than 59 1/2) from those accounts, unless the funds are in a Roth account. However, you must still take future tax implications into account when considering how to divide tax-deferred retirement vehicles. $100K in a 401(k) is pre-tax money, and it is not worth as much as $100K in a bank account on which taxes have already been paid.

Pay careful attention to the wording of your settlement agreement. With stocks, the dates, decimals and details all matter.

Suppose your divorce settlement agreement states specifically that you are to receive $100K out of a $200K stock portfolio. Remember that the value of stock is always changing. What if, by the time the portfolio gets divided, the investments are worth $250K? Well, even if the original intent was for you to get half its value, you'd still get only get $100K, because that's what you agreed to.

If the intention of the agreement is for you to get half, then make sure the divorce settlement agreement says half, and don't specify a dollar amount.

Of course, this goes both ways: If the investments are on the decline and it's important to be sure you get a certain amount of money, then be sure your agreement states that amount exactly, and not a percentage.

Wording can affect the valuation of stocks, as well. Why? Because, once again, the value of a stock can change over time.

> *Remember: Since the value of some assets can fluctuate over time, assets must be assigned a value on a particular date in order to calculate how they will be divided, and the point in time at which a particular asset is assigned a dollar value is called its Valuation Date. (See Volume I, Chapter 11 for more about Valuation Dates.)*

If a couple does go to court, there can be broad discretion in deciding the date of valuation. For example, while the Date of Separation and Valuation Dates may be the same for some assets, they can be different for others. In addition, while some assets may be valued when litigation begins, the court can make adjustments if these assets appreciate or depreciate between the time the litigation starts and when the divorce is finally granted. As you can imagine, this can become extremely complicated, particularly if there is a long delay between the dates of separation and divorce.

And there's even one more wrinkle you need to understand. You see, although each state has its own specific regulations and guidelines for determining the Valuation Date of an asset, typically the Valuation Date is determined by whether or not the asset is active or passive.

» An **active asset** is any marital property that can change in value due to the actions of its owner. For instance, a business, a professional practice, and even the marital home can be considered active assets.

» A **passive asset**, on the other hand, is any marital property that can change value because of forces beyond the direct control of its owner. For example, vacant land and stock portfolios (unless actively managed) may be considered passive assets because their value depends on market forces.

Active assets are typically valued as of the Date of Separation or commencement date of the action, while passive assets are usually valued as of the trial date.

Now that you've got a handle on how to approach the division of stock in your divorce, take that know-how forward into your life as a single woman. As soon as your divorce is final and the dust settles, meet with a qualified financial advisor to expand or adjust your investment portfolio for continued financial benefit. (Look for my book, *Think Financially, Not Emotionally*® - *A Woman's Guide To Financial Security After Divorce*[3], to be published in late 2015.)

 Reminder: If you have stock that you've inherited or received as a gift from a third party, and it has not been commingled with investments or accounts that you share with your husband, then that stock could well be considered separate property, in most states. (Note: Even though in most states your husband cannot claim any part of your separate property, he might be able to claim appreciation in value if that increase was due to your active management of that portfolio and not just outside market forces.)

Hot tip: If your stock was inherited, or given to you many years ago, it can be difficult to determine its cost basis. There are online tools for calculating cost basis, and the more information you have, the more reliable the result. The date the stock was purchased is important to know. Without a documented cost basis, you may be required to use $0, which can be very expensive at tax time, as the stock's entire current value will be considered a capital gain. This is a good case for seeking expert financial advice.

Legal matters: Dividing a complex stock portfolio to your best advantage may well be outside your divorce attorney's scope of expertise. Don't expect your legal expert to be your financial expert (or vice versa).

FOUR DIFFICULTIES TO AVOID WHEN DIVIDING STOCK OPTIONS AND RESTRICTED STOCK IN DIVORCE

Many affluent couples have exceedingly complicated financial portfolios to split when they divorce. If you and your soon-to-be-ex-husband cannot agree on the value of your houses and vehicles, it won't be easy to divide assets with values that are uncertain—and potentially enormous! Stock options and restricted stock fall into this category, and can be some of the most difficult assets to divide fairly.

In the previous chapter, I discussed how stock is divided in divorce. Now, let me point out a few common pitfalls divorcing women encounter when dividing stock options and restricted stock. First, though, let's back up a bit and define what these assets are.

» **Stock options** give an employee the right to buy a specific amount of company stock at a set price, at a future date. The idea is that this set price will be considerably lower than the future trading price, so that the employee can then sell their cheaply bought stock at great profit. That is called "exercising" the options.

» **Restricted stock** refers to company shares that are granted at no cost to employees, but that are not transferable until certain conditions, such as employment by the company for a specified period of time, have been met. When the conditions are met, the stock is said to have "vested."

Stock options and restricted stock can be hugely valuable. This is especially true at promising start-up companies, which may be long on potential but short on available funds. And while not everyone is going to cash in on a scale that makes national news, the employee's hope is that in return for some lean years early on, they will one day be made very wealthy indeed. In short, stock options and restricted stock are compensation based on an implied promise of future riches . . . but with no guarantees.

As these types of assets are becoming more and more common in employee compensation packages, they are naturally becoming more and more common in divorce settlement negotiations, as well. If this applies to you, please take note of these four pitfalls to avoid when dividing stock options or restricted stock in divorce:

Not knowing the options/stock exist in the first place.

Maybe your husband was a hardworking young professional who helped get a tech start-up off the ground, and early in your marriage, the two of you decided together that taking stock options or restricted stock as part of his compensation package would be a good move. In that case, you're aware of the assets, though they may have been augmented over the years in ways you didn't know about or keep track of.

However, a divorcing woman definitely shouldn't take for granted that she would know about her husband's stock options or restricted stock. These assets would not typically appear on tax returns, W-2 forms, or other financial documentation, unless and until the options are actually exercised and the restricted stock has vested.

Have your attorney make special efforts to determine whether your husband is holding stock options or restricted stock, and what the timetable is for being able to exercise the options/sell the stock. Given that you're divorcing, you might not want to rely on your husband to willingly disclose such things.

Not knowing what the options/stock are worth.

While a quick internet search can reveal the current value of stock options and restricted stock for many publicly traded companies, it can be much harder to determine the current value of stock options and restricted stock for a privately held company. Before the options are exercised and the stock is sold, nobody knows how much they will actually turn out to be worth. And without knowing that, of course you can't precisely assess what your fair share would be.

Compounding the difficulty, the issue is treated differently in different states.

In some states, if the stock options/restricted stock have not vested as of the Date of Separation[1], they are not considered marital property. In other states they are, but their current value depends on factors such as how far in the future they vest. This is easier to compute with restricted stocks, because unless the company goes bankrupt, the stock should have some value. Stock options, however, could have an exercise (strike) price that is greater than its current market value (a condition commonly referred to as "being under water").

I asked Memphis Divorce Lawyer and Family Law Attorney Miles Mason, Sr.[2], Esq., CPA, for his advice. "In my experience, employee spouses with 'under water' stock options often claim the value for marital property division to be zero, but even if the exercise price is less than the market price of the stock, options can have tremendous value in the future if (or when) the market price exceeds the exercise price," he told me. "When faced with this situation at the divorce negotiating table, I use an example to make the point that even under water options can have value. I offer $20.00 cash to the employee spouse for the stock options. Of course, the employee spouse turns my offer down. Then, I offer $100.00. Again, my offer is always rejected. Ultimately, the point is made.

We recommend clients utilize a forensic accountant or economist to discuss the potential value over time. At the end of the day, negotiating value for under water stock options is part science and part art. The result of the negotiation may likely depend on the value placed on the options' ownership by the employee spouse which could be based partly on knowledge of the companies' performance and partly based on unpredictable emotion."

Not getting your fair share.

You now know how difficult it can be to determine your fair share of stock options and restricted stock. You will need a highly qualified divorce financial advisor[3] to work through all the angles involved in determining what's "fair," and an experienced attorney to make sure your settlement includes it.

If, in the end, you opt not to receive a share of the stock options/restricted stock, be sure your portfolio will include assets that are equally likely to appreciate at least as much, and with no worse tax consequences.

Not anticipating the tax consequences.

Taxes on profits from exercising stock options or selling restricted stock are significant, and should factor in to your assessment of the worth of these assets in your settlement. Although you should always rely on your accountant for the most current tax information, here are a few fundamentals for you to consider:

Income from exercising "qualified" options, such as ISOs (Incentive Stock Options), which can only be granted to employees, is generally taxed as capital gains, not ordinary income, provided the options are held for two years after the grant date or one year after the exercise date, whichever is later.

On the other hand, income from "nonqualified" options is generally subject to standard income tax rates, and when nonqualified stock options are exercised, the difference between the market price and the strike price will be taxed as ordinary income. If those shares are then sold, any gain or loss will be taxed as short-term if held for less than one year, and long-term if held for more than one year.

Restricted stock is taxed as ordinary income upon vesting.

You now know you need to determine whether there are stock and/or options that need to be divided in your divorce, develop an estimate of their value, and assess how much will be part of your settlement and what the wisest tax strategy will be for handling them. Next, you will need a plan for turning this "paper wealth" into cash. As with all things financial, make sure you have expert advice to follow through on this last step. Then, move on and enjoy the benefits you gain from being prepared!

Reminder: You should make every effort to find out what stock options/restricted stock are included in your husband's compensation package. If you have reason to believe these assets might exist, but can't prove it, your attorney may be able to subpoena his company's human resources records.

Hot tip: The terms of stock options and restricted stock in compensation packages sometimes prohibit transfer of these assets to a spouse. If that is your situation, your ex would have to exercise the options and/or sell the stock on your behalf. In those cases, the proceeds would be taxed at your ex's tax rate.

Legal matters: If you believe your husband might be hiding assets or being less than truthful in any aspect of your divorce, do not use mediation or collaborative divorce to arrive at a settlement agreement. With both mediation and collaborative divorce, you surrender the ability to subpoena records, and would have to accept your husband's word on the existence (or not) of restricted stock or stock options in his portfolio.

CHAPTER 18

DON'T CUT THE REMBRANDT IN HALF! HOW TO DIVIDE ART AND OTHER DIFFICULT-TO-DIVIDE ASSETS

D ivorce involves the division of marital property[1] . . . and that means *all* marital property. The cars, the house, the vacation condo—even the new HD TV, the patio furniture, and the flatware your grandmother gave you both as an anniversary gift years ago—all marital assets like these must be divided according to the rules in your state[2].

For some marital property, the process is relatively easy. Maybe you'll happily part with that monstrous TV? Perhaps he has no interest in your family's heirloom silver? Backed by a qualified divorce team[3], you can work through all those nitty-gritty details, and generally, negotiations about marital assets can proceed in a productive and timely fashion (for the most part).

In other cases, however, the process is anything but smooth. Some couples own difficult-to-divide assets, such as art collections and huge, multi-faceted business entities. Are you worried about what will happen to the paintings you purchased during all those European vacations? How can you split ownership of your favorite horses? Is there any way to divide something as complex as, say, a business franchise you and your husband own together?

If your divorce involves difficult-to-divide marital assets, please keep these key factors top-of-mind:

» **Not all assets that are valued the same are actually *worth* the same.** At first, that sentence may sound somewhat confusing, but let me use an example involving a marital residence to illustrate my point:

Let's say you're trying to decide whether to keep a $600,000 bank account or a $600,000 house that's completely paid off. You really love the house, and you're leaning in that direction. But, is keeping the house the best financial decision for you? That depends! Before deciding one way or another, you need to carefully assess how the house will impact your bottom line—both now and years down the road. Even mortgage-free home ownership involves expenses, such as real estate taxes that need to be paid every year, upkeep and maintenance, fuel costs, etc.

In addition, when you eventually sell your home you may be hit with a big capital gains tax bill. Let's assume you bought the home for $200,000, and it's now worth $600,000. Your capital gain is $400,000. Subtract your $250,000 capital gains exclusion as a single person, and you would have to pay capital gains tax on $150,000.

What would those capital gains taxes be? Thanks to the changes in tax laws[4] in 2013, if your taxable income is greater than $400,000, your federal capital gains tax rate has increased from 15 percent to 20 percent. As a result, if you fall into that higher tax bracket, you'll have to pay $30,000 in capital gains tax (20 percent of $150,000 is $30,000)—plus, a new additional 3.8 percent Medicare surtax of $5,700 tax on those gains (3.8 percent of $150,000 is $5,700), *plus* your state's capital gains taxes.

Once you complete this type of analysis, the $600,000 bank account may look like a much better option than the house!

» **Liquidating assets so you can split the proceeds is not necessarily easy or the most viable option.** Sometimes the tax implications and/or other associated costs of selling certain assets outweigh the benefits of liquidation. Make sure you fully understand all potential financial consequences before you agree to "sell it all."

On the other hand . . .

» **To *Think Financially, Not Emotionally*®5 is *always* optimal.** I understand that you may not want to live without your beachfront getaway, that antique watch, or the impressionist painting you see every evening in the dining room. But the truth is this: *You can.* I'm not saying you have to; I'm saying you *can*.

I understand that maintaining emotional distance when it comes to negotiating certain assets may not be easy. But if you can successfully do so, you'll put yourself in a better position to strategically manage your marital property and develop a comprehensive plan for financial stability and security in the future.

Reminder: States differ in some of the details, but typically, all property acquired during the marriage is considered **marital property**, regardless of which spouse owns the property or how the property is titled. By contrast, separate property is property owned by either spouse prior to the marriage or after the Date of Separation. Separate property can also include inheritances, gifts, or other special personal injury awards received by one spouse or the other. (See Chapter 15 of this book and Volume I, Chapter 9 for more details about the difference between marital property and separate property.)

Hot tip: Legal documents such as pre-nuptial agreements, post-nuptial agreements, and trusts help clarify who owns what. So, as I've said many times before, when it comes to marriage and assets, your best offense is a good defense.

Even though the thought of divorce may be the furthest thing from your mind while you are drafting an agreement, it's essential that you consider "the possibility" of a future breakup while you are establishing the terms. Will your assets be protected from your husband (or other unanticipated recipient) if you divorce? Are the proper safeguards in place?

Legal matters: Understanding the difference between separate and marital property is only the first step in approaching the division of family property. You must also recognize that divorce laws differ greatly from state to state. You need to know if you live in a Community Property State or an Equitable Distribution State because where you live impacts how your assets and debts will be divided during divorce.

CHAPTER 19

HOW PETS ARE HANDLED IN DIVORCE

When custody issues arise in divorce, they almost always concern children. But often, there's another member of the family whose care and housing also needs to be considered and decided when a married couple parts ways: the family pet.

Most of the time, the question of pet custody and care is settled out of court, and usually, the answer is obvious. If you and your husband agree that "she's always been more your cat anyway," or "the dog really belongs with the kids," there's really no dilemma. Sometimes, it's recognized that neither spouse can properly care for a pet independently, so the animal is found a new home entirely.

What happens in the opposite situation, when both spouses claim to want custody of the pet?

Divorce can be an emotionally vulnerable time under the best of circumstances, and arguing over a treasured animal friend can compound the difficulty (and sadness) of the whole experience. So, with about 62% of American households including at least one pet[1], and about 50% of American marriages ending in divorce[2], perhaps it's no surprise that pet custody cases are coming before divorce court judges more and more often.

The first thing to understand about pets in divorce is that while you may consider your furry friend a member of the family, in the eyes of the law he is almost always personal property, plain and simple, just like paintings and patio furniture. (Note: If you or your spouse breed and sell animals, your pets might also be considered business assets. Some purebreds sell for significant sums.)

Naturally, though, a pet is not the kind of property that can be divided 50/50. Here are some of the questions a court might consider in deciding pet custody cases:

Whose pet is it?

If the pet belonged to either spouse before the marriage, the case is much clearer that it should belong to that same spouse after the divorce.

Who cares for the pet?

Who buys the pet food and supplies? Who takes the pet to the veterinarian for check-ups, or if it's hurt? Who feeds it, walks it, cleans up after it? (Interestingly, dogs are reportedly the most frequently disputed family animal; cats are a distant second.)

Where are the children going to live?

If there are children involved, and the pet is truly a family pet, then sometimes it is best for everyone to have the pet live with the kids. If custody of the children is shared, perhaps custody of the dog can be shared, too. (I have a feeling this wouldn't go over so well with cats, but stranger things have happened.)

After the divorce, whose life will be better suited to pet ownership?

Pets benefit from consistency and lots of positive interaction with their humans. If one of you works long hours and travels often and on short notice, while the other works from home or has a more predictable schedule, it is pretty clear whose lifestyle is better suited to providing a good environment for a pet.

Those all seem like reasonable questions, and fairly easy to answer, if all parties behave honorably.

Unfortunately, that's not always the case. Unscrupulous soon-to-be-ex-spouses have been known to try to use the family pet as a bargaining chip in divorce. If you have a strong emotional attachment to your pet, your husband likely knows it—and may try to use it against you. Knowing you would be devastated to lose the pet, your husband might threaten to pursue custody himself, hoping that you'll concede something with significant financial value to get him to drop the demand.

If your husband is using your pet to try to force your hand in the divorce process, a common sense strategy can fight this tactic. The facts may be on your side.

Look again at the list of questions, above, and with those in mind, gather evidence to prove that you should have custody of your pet. Here are some ways to build your case:

» Ask your vet to sign a simple statement acknowledging that it is you, not your husband, who brings the animal in for check-ups and treatments.

» Ask neighbors to attest to the fact that it is you who regularly walks the dog.

» Save pet supply store receipts with your signature on them.

» Who signed the application for the dog license . . . was that you, too? Get a copy from your city clerk.

» Cite the differences in your husband's work schedule and yours that make you a better choice to keep your pet.

These things can all go to show that as primary (or sole!) caretaker of your beloved animal, you deserve to have him live with you after your divorce. Prepare a well-reasoned, factual statement to accompany your documentation and make your case to keep your pet.

Divorce takes place in a dog-eat-dog world . . . but remember, judges have pets, too. If your husband is blatantly exploiting your emotional bond with a pet in order to wrangle something else out of you, he should be prepared for a judge to call that out for the nasty, underhanded tactic it is.

Reminder: It's very hard to *Think Financially, Not Emotionally*[®3] about your pet. There's no dollar value to be placed on the benefits of pet ownership[4]. Women should be aware that their husbands might try to use that to their advantage and be prepared with a strategy of their own.

Hot tip: Many pet owners today purchase health insurance for their pets. If you and your husband have a pet health insurance policy, be sure that your settlement agreement specifies who will be responsible for paying those premiums.

Legal matters: Because a pet is usually legally considered personal property, you may be able to use a prenuptial agreement[5] to ensure that your pet will stay yours, no matter what happens in the future of your marriage. If it's past time for a prenup, consider including provisions for your pet(s) in a postnuptial agreement.

CHAPTER 20

WHO GETS THE AIR MILES?

Frequent, prolonged travel can strain a marriage—and if the marriage ends in divorce, it can also present a unique question in settlement negotiations. When you're dividing marital assets, who gets the frequent flyer miles?

At first, that might seem like a joke. Why would anyone quibble about something as trivial as air miles? But think about it. Imagine, for example, a Boston couple in which the husband works for a California bank and spends the first week of every month in San Francisco. He flies the same airline and stays in the same luxury hotel on every trip . . . and has been doing so for almost 20 years. Or think of a New York executive who flies frequently to his company's international headquarters in Geneva. We all know people whose careers involve travel, and for them, reward program point totals are not at all trivial. On the contrary, they can add up to significant benefits when redeemed.

In working towards a divorce settlement agreement, if you can train yourself to *Think Financially, Not Emotionally*®[1], you will come to see all marital assets as items to be negotiated in terms of their value in dollars and cents. Initially, you'll work through the obvious physical assets: houses and other real estate, cars, boats, etc. Then, you'll cover insurance policies, stock portfolios, and retirement plans. You'll even hash out the value of collections and other unusual assets—everything from race horses to rare coins can be appraised, and their value divided.

It's the same with air miles or other reward points. The key to negotiating who gets them is not the number of points, but their dollar value.

The first step in assessing how to divide air miles and reward points is to read the terms and conditions of your various rewards programs. I realize this can be some of the most tedious fine print imaginable, but it may give you definitive answers. Take Marriott's reward program, for example. Its 2014 Conditions of Enrollment specify[2] that points are not transferable to a spouse as part of a divorce. Rather than trying to maneuver around this provision with a court order, it probably makes more sense to assign a value to those points and negotiate for something of equivalent value in your settlement, instead.

Assigning a cash value to loyalty program points—whether they're from an airline, a hotel chain, or a credit card—can be tricky. "Loyalty currency" simply doesn't translate into cash currency in any standard or straightforward way. If your travel program doesn't provide a cash value equivalent for its points, you may have to do a rough conversion of miles or points into trips or other rewards, and then estimate the value of those, in turn.

For instance, if an airline requires 50,000 bonus miles to be redeemed for a first class ticket that would cost $1,500, you can reasonably estimate $1,500 as the cash value of the 50,000 miles. Keep in mind that the value could vary depending on the destination and time of year. Don't use an outrageous maximum value that could be denied outright and damage your credibility. Do some research and come up with a value that's both realistic and defensible.

Another strategy, if the company awarding the points will allow it, is simply to have the airline or other reward-granting program divide the points equally into two separate accounts. If you go this route, remember that there will likely be fees incurred for transferring the points and/or resetting their expiration dates. Have a plan for handling the fees as fairly as you're handling the bonus points.

People can be very possessive of their travel rewards points. If you're like me, you store up the miles for a time when you can use them for a truly pleasurable trip. That trip becomes something to look forward to, and having that taken away can leave you feeling cheated, or even robbed.

At the end of the day, though, when negotiating your divorce settlement, all air miles and other loyalty program reward points really come down to money. If you *Think Financially, Not Emotionally*®³, you may discover that giving up the air miles in favor of another consideration elsewhere can be a smart financial move—particularly if those miles and points are near expiration!

Reminder: Don't ignore air miles when listing marital assets. With frequent travel, bonus points can stack up quickly. It's not unheard of for frequent flyers to accumulate more than a million air miles!

Hot tip: If your husband reports that the loyalty program "owns" the bonus points, not him, he may be right. But even so, the points have value, and *that's* what you're negotiating for. When you ask for an asset of equivalent worth instead of the points themselves, think of several reasonable alternatives, and be sure the value of each represents a smart trade-off for you.

Legal matters: If comparing and contrasting the enrollment terms of multiple travel and credit card bonus point plans are more than you want to undertake, then ask your attorney specifically about their experience with dividing loyalty points. There's a good chance the firm has handled the issue before and is familiar with the various restrictions in place.

CHAPTER 21

ARE YOUR STUDENT LOANS SEPARATE OR MARITAL DEBT?

A s I've mentioned in the previous chapters, the division of assets is a hot topic in every divorce. It's the meat of the matter, so to speak, and every woman wants to walk away with at least her fair share.

However, the other side of the coin—the division of debt—deserves just as much attention. (Even though, as you might imagine, it's typically much less desirable to have debt included in a divorce settlement agreement!)

Before you get to strategies for maximizing assets and minimizing debt, you need to have a solid understanding of how these things are divided (or not), according to the laws of your state. In Chapter 15 (and in Volume I, Chapter 9), I reviewed the differences between separate and marital property[1].

You must also understand that how your marital property will be divided depends on whether you live in a "Community Property" State or an "Equitable Distribution" State[2].

In **Community Property States,** spouses are considered equal owners of all marital property, and assets are split 50-50 during a divorce.

In **Equitable Distribution States** (most states are in this category), the division of marital assets is more complicated than that. No matter which spouse is listed as the owner of a given asset, each spouse has a legal claim to a fair and equitable portion of its value. Remember, though: "fair and equitable" doesn't necessarily mean "half." Courts consider many factors to determine what constitutes a fair and equitable distribution of marital property. (See Volume I, Chapter 8 for a more complete discussion of the difference between Community Property States and Equitable Distribution States.)

That's assets. How does it go with debt? As a married couple, you may be holding credit card debt, car loans, mortgages, personal loans, business loans and, as we'll now discuss further, debt from financing your education and/or your husband's.

Student debt is an increasingly significant piece of the marital financial picture for many couples these days, especially among younger couples. It's not uncommon for professionals with multiple advanced degrees to be carrying student debt reaching well into six figures! So, who is responsible for paying student loans incurred during the marriage? Are student loans considered separate, or marital debt?

In divorce, debt is generally divided using the same principles that are used to divide assets. Let me walk you through the answers to four questions that come into play when dividing student loan debt in Equitable Distribution States, where "fair and equitable" is the standard.

1. **What did the loan actually pay for?**

   When a student loan is used for tuition, school fees, books, etc. in pursuit of a degree earned by one spouse, it's simpler to make the case that the loan represents the separate debt of that spouse. However, couples often use the borrowed money for living expenses or other costs—and understandably, this can muddy the waters. If it's not clear that your or your husband's student loan was used specifically for education, it will more likely be considered marital debt from which both spouses benefitted, and for which both spouses are logically responsible.

2. **If the loan paid for a degree earned, does your state consider the degree to be separate property or marital property?**

   If the money borrowed was used toward earning a professional degree, and the degree is the separate property of one spouse, then the debt is more clearly considered separate. However, in a few states, such as New York, professional degrees are (perhaps counterintuitively) considered to be marital property (if earned during the marriage) . . . and debt incurred to obtain marital property is more likely to be considered marital debt.

3. **What is the earning power of each spouse at the time of divorce?**
Part of calculating "equitable distribution" is assessing each spouse's ability to support themselves and their dependents. For example, if you have no significant income or earning potential of your own at the time of divorce (even though you may have had both when you were first married), it's less likely to be considered fair for you to be saddled with your ex-husband's student loan payments.

It may be advisable to consult with a vocational expert[3] to assess your earning potential in the current job market and to quantify how much your professional degree paid for by the student loan contributes to that earning potential.

4. **Who has benefitted from the degree-earner's earning power, and for how long?**
In dividing student loan debt during divorce, the key question is not who incurred the debt,

but who benefitted from it. If the divorce happens soon after graduation, a student loan is more likely to be considered separate debt, because the other spouse has not had much time to benefit from the degree-earner's earning power. However, if the loan made possible a substantial income from which both spouses benefitted over many years, that's a convincing case for considering any outstanding student loan balance to be marital debt.

How can you protect yourself from being saddled with debt you don't believe to be rightly yours? Use a well-conceived, properly-executed prenuptial agreement[4] to lay out the expectation for ownership of the debt *before* you get married. If you have a prenup that doesn't cover student loan debt, see if you can get a postnuptial agreement drafted to rectify that. (Note: Only a postnup can amend a prenup once you are married.) Or, if you never had a prenup, you might consider a postnup before taking on student loans during the marriage. You can use the postnup to specify how student loan debt would be paid in the event of a break-up.

Reminder: If you live in a Community Property State, most debts incurred during the marriage are considered joint debts, and you will likely be liable for half.

Hot tip: There are often tax and other financial consequences to assuming (or paying off) debt (For example, as of this writing, student loans are still not dismissible in bankruptcy). Depending on your particular circumstances, those tax and other consequences could be positive or negative financially. Make sure you check with your accountant for the most current tax information and to learn how your taxes could be impacted by your student loan(s).

Legal matters: While the number of cases on record is growing daily, court decisions about the division of student loan debt in divorce are not entirely consistent. If student debt makes up a significant fraction of the debt in your marital financial portfolio, ask your attorney specifically how it has been regarded by the family court in your jurisdiction.

CHAPTER 22

WHEN PARENTS DIVORCE, WHO PAYS FOR COLLEGE?

Paying college tuition for one or more children is among the biggest financial challenges for today's parents. When the parents are married, it's difficult enough; when the parents have split up, it's even worse. For example, divorced parents face emotionally charged complications around not just how to plan for college tuition and related expenses, but also who, exactly, is going to be paying for those substantial bills.

In many cases, child support payments cease when children reach the "age of emancipation," which in most states is between 18 and 21, precisely when you'll need to be financing their higher education. Whether your children are still young or already applying to colleges, this represents a whole suite of things to keep in mind when negotiating your divorce settlement agreement.

Here are the most important things to consider:

Your divorce settlement should specifically include a written college support agreement, in addition to any other child support agreements.

A college support agreement can set forth in detail what percentage of college expenses each parent is responsible for, any limits on payments or restrictions on which college the child should attend, exactly what expenses will be covered, etc.

Each one of these provisions usually has to be negotiated. Establishing limits to payments can be especially problematic, and may involve intricate calculations and stipulations. In New York State, for instance, many divorcing parents agree to limit their contribution according to what's known as the "SUNY Cap." This cap limits a parent's obligation to a percentage of the cost of a State University of New York (SUNY) school. In other words, regardless of where the child attends college, if the SUNY Cap is applied, the parent is obligated to pay only that specified amount. (Parents in other states may agree to limits based on their own state schools' tuition rates.)

An up-front, lump sum payment may be preferable to recurring payments.

As part of your settlement agreement, you can have funds put into an escrow or trust account to make sure they are available when needed for college, or get an up-front lump sum payment.

Particularly if your child is young, it may be preferable to negotiate an up-front, lump sum payment to cover college expenses, assuming there are sufficient assets available. Then, when your child reaches college age, you'll have these funds in hand to help pay the tuition bills, provided you have put the money aside and invested it wisely.

Certain custody arrangements can complicate things.

Division of college expenses can be especially complicated if custody is split such that one parent has custody of one child (or some children), and the other has custody of another (or others).

In general, courts want to see that the numbers balance, and that one parent is not unfairly burdened with college-related costs. Variables such as how much each parent earns, the tuition expenses, and other child care costs are factored into the equation.

If applicable terms have not been included in your settlement agreement, the courts can order a parent to pay for their child's education—but it depends on the state in which the divorce occurs.

Most states allow courts to order the non-custodial parent to help pay for college. But a few, like Alaska, Nebraska, and New Hampshire, do not, except in those cases where the parents had a previous agreement.

Typically, though, even in the states that don't require paying for college expenses, the courts do recognize the need for children to have a college education. Therefore, they can allow resolution of the issue to be part of the divorce settlement agreement, in addition to the amount and term of alimony and child support to be paid.

Keep in mind that unless ordered by the courts, there is *no legal obligation* for a parent to pay college tuition.

Without a court order, the only way to secure funds for college tuition is to include the obligation in your divorce settlement agreement. It is well worth your time and effort to negotiate and agree now how your children's college expenses will be paid when the time comes.

Once the question of expenses is settled, you're free to enjoy the thrill of your children's acceptance to college, and take pride in their first step into the wider, adult world.

Reminder: College costs don't stop at tuition. Plan for fees, room and board, extracurricular activities, books, computer/printer, transportation, and an allowance. Even though you may not feel up to the additional wrangling, it's important to negotiate now who will pay for each of these things later.

Hot tip: Estimating future college costs can be very difficult, especially if your children are still young. Most divorce attorneys don't have the training or expertise to accurately project future college costs and then calculate what the present value of those costs would be in today's dollars for inclusion in your divorce settlement agreement. A consultation with a divorce financial advisor[1] can help you better understand all the options available, and help you plan for a secure financial future for you and your children.

Legal matters: Courts have broad jurisdiction in the area of caps on tuition obligations, and have sometimes concluded that there is no basis for them. Before you agree to a cap, consult with an attorney familiar with the legal climate in your state, including any relevant legislation in the works.

3

PROTECTING YOUR ASSETS

Volume I incudes chapters about alimony, hidden assets, whether or not you should keep your house, and how your divorce will impact your retirement accounts, pension plans, insurance policies, Social Security, intellectual property, etc. The chapters in this section of Volume II are devoted to additional things you need to know to protect your assets, including what can happen if your husband lies about his finances, whether or not you should litigate or settle, how to make sure you actually receive the child support and alimony you're owed, and how to use a QDRO to enforce the financial terms of your divorce settlement.

CHAPTER 23

WHY YOU NEED TO KNOW PRECISELY WHAT YOUR HUSBAND EARNS IN HIS CASH-BASED BUSINESS

In an ideal world, you and your husband would want only the best for each other as you make your way through divorce proceedings. Both sides would be completely open and honest, and in the end, you'd politely part ways, each satisfied with the negotiated settlement.

But, in the real world, we all know "friendly" break-ups are rare. Even in relatively amicable splits, each spouse needs to protect his/her interests to be sure the settlement is fair . . . and naturally, this is especially critical for the less-monied, or supported spouse—who even today, is most often the wife.

As I often remind my clients, the goal of your divorce process is not only to put a legal end to your marriage so that you can move on with your life. The

goal of your divorce process must also include the negotiation of a fair settlement agreement, so that when you ***do*** move on, you'll have a financial footing that's as rock solid as possible.

Will spousal support be part of your divorce settlement agreement? Quite possibly, it will . . . and in order to receive what you deserve, you need to have a detailed understanding of what your husband earns. How much do you really know about his income? If he owns his own business, have you ever been completely certain about what he earns?

Let me walk you through some of the fundamentals of spousal support and why you need to be especially vigilant if your husband owns his own business.

Spousal support is determined using a variety of factors.

There is no precise "formula" for calculating spousal support, and the courts have fairly wide discretion over how it is determined. For example, the judge may consider (or choose not to consider) a variety of factors, including:

» the income and property of each spouse
» earning capacity of each spouse
» impairments in earning capacity
» whether there are any children (and who will be raising them)
» standard of living during the marriage

» age and health of each spouse
» education and training of each spouse
» duration of the marriage
» sacrifices or contributions one spouse made to the career and/or education of the other.

Since determining spousal support is far from an "exact science," different judges in the same jurisdiction can come up with wildly different determinations—even when presented with similar sets of circumstances. (Note: This is another reason to stay out of court, if at all possible!)

Typically, your husband's income plays a very significant role in the determination of spousal support—and that's precisely why determining how much he earns should be an early and major responsibility of your divorce team[1].

Sometimes, it's a straightforward task, involving little more than an examination of his pay stubs and tax returns. However, the process can be significantly more complicated when sources like these don't seem to tell the whole story.

If your husband owns his own business, and especially if a high percentage of the business income is in cash, it can be extremely difficult to determine his true income.

Why? Because cash can easily be hidden[2]. For instance, cash is often used to buy luxury items that can add significantly to a person's net worth, without ever having been reported to the IRS as income.

Miles Mason, Sr.[3], Esq., a Memphis divorce lawyer and CPA of long experience, has written a book about divorce litigation involving complex financial assets[4]. He notes:

Cars, boats, and even second homes can be purchased with income obtained with secreted cash. Restaurant and bar owners, lawn-service companies, and painting and drywall subcontractors are all often paid by customers with cash, which is often not reported on tax returns. (Unfortunately, some lawyers even transact business this way.) Understanding the type of business and how it is transacted is one key to investigating an unexplained increase in net worth. Some spouses of business owners may have a clue about this tax fraud and whether it occurs on a regular basis. During the marriage, there may have been a time when cash was paid for items in the presence of the non-business-owner spouse, and the owner may have even bragged about this particular shortcut "saving" money on taxes.

If this sounds familiar, you should assume your husband will use the same tactic during your divorce. He may try to hide cash in order to appear as though he can't afford much spousal or child support.

You need to learn "as much as possible" about your husband's business.

If you have a good sense of the business income and expenses, assets and debts and how it is run financially, you will be sharply attuned to whether your husband is underreporting his income in the divorce process. You'll know where to look for cash flows he might have neglected to mention. The more you know about the business operation, the sooner and more accurately you'll sense wrongdoing if his income documentation doesn't say what it should.

The opportunity to squirrel away cash exists in nearly *every* job, not just the ones that typically see a lot of cash transactions.

College professors may take consulting jobs outside the classroom. Doctors' practices may pay for their cars. Think about whether your husband has had those kinds of side jobs or material benefits over the course of your marriage, and then think about whether they have been reported as income.

A carefully prepared, comprehensive Lifestyle Analysis will help you better understand his income.

In essence, a Lifestyle Analysis[5] establishes what your standard of living was during the marriage. It reconstructs the day-to-day living expenses incurred during the marriage and the spending habits of both you and your husband. When prepared by a qualified divorce financial advisor[6], a Lifestyle Analysis will alert you to the possibility your husband is trying to hide and/or dissipate marital assets. (See Chapter 14 for more about why a Lifestyle Analysis is so important.)

For example, if the Lifestyle Analysis shows that the lifestyle exceeds the reported income, the extra money can only have come from:

» bank, brokerage, and other accounts
» loans/debt
» sale of assets
» gifts or
» unreported income and/or assets

Once you have a clear understanding of what your husband earns you'll be better able to negotiate a fair divorce settlement agreement—one that will enable you to move on with confidence to a more financially secure future as an independent woman.

Reminder: If your husband owns his own business, you need to know as much as you can about the financial aspects of his work. To that end, a Lifestyle Analysis[7] is a good first step, and it can help ensure you will receive the most equitable distribution of assets possible and a reasonable amount of alimony for a reasonable amount of time.

Hot tip: If the evidence suggests your husband's records are incomplete, inaccurate or downright fraudulent, your divorce team will have to construct a likely picture of his "true" income. This process is called imputing income and may require the talents of a forensic accountant. These highly specialized accountants like nothing better than to piece together true income and net worth from documentation that deliberately does not show the complete picture.

Legal matters: Don't confuse child support with spousal support. Child support is determined based on a formula that varies from state to state. Spousal support, on the other hand, is dependent on a variety of factors, and the courts have fairly wide discretion on how it is determined.

CHAPTER 24

WATCH OUT FOR SUDDEN INCOME DEFICIT SYNDROME (SIDS)

All married women benefit from being fully aware of and involved with family finances. If your marriage is thriving, managing your finances as a team makes for an equal partnership and gives you the confidence of knowing that either one of you is capable of steering the ship. And when your marriage isn't thriving, it's even more important to have a good handle on your marital financial circumstances. I realize that at first, it may seem easiest to leave all the "money stuff" to someone else; but when it comes to divorce, ignorance is *not* bliss . . . and it can be very costly, indeed.

Think about it: When divorce is on the horizon, it's only natural for each spouse to begin to jealously guard his/her own financial self-interest—whether that means trying to make sure that assets are divided equitably in a settlement, or trying to make sure that they're not. The sad truth is that husbands are typically much quicker than wives to assume a financially self-protective stance, and so if you don't know the extent of your marital assets, you may be vulnerable to the financial maneuvering[1] that many husbands do to minimize their losses in divorce.

For instance, as I mentioned in the previous chapter, owning a business presents several opportunities for these kinds of dirty tricks. Have you been financially supported in proud style by your husband's business throughout your marriage? Don't be taken aback, once divorce proceedings start, to hear that—surprise!—the business actually has little or no income or value.

This sudden-onset poverty, conveniently timed to ensure your husband can't afford to pay a fair settlement, is so common that it has an admittedly cynical name among divorce professionals. We call it Sudden Income Deficit Syndrome (SIDS).

Is your husband likely to come down with a case of SIDS—and more importantly, are *your* finances at risk from his affliction? Watch for these clues:

» **He hasn't bought himself anything nice in a while, which isn't like him. He even traded the Mercedes for a Volkswagen!**
   Some husbands will try to take the "sudden" out of "Sudden Income Deficit Syndrome" by attempting to establish credibility for their claims of dire financial straits. As soon as the

marriage hits the rocks, they'll set the stage for SIDS by paring down personal income from the business and setting aside luxuries. After the divorce is settled to their advantage, they'll give back the economy car, move out of the low-rent apartment, and resume their previous lifestyle.

Miles Mason, Sr., Esq., CPA, founder of Miles Mason Family Law Group[2] and the author of *The Tennessee Divorce Client's Handbook: What Every Divorcing Spouse Needs to Know*[3], has seen this tactic in action.

"Divorce lawyers also see some craftier business owners start poor-mouthing the business profitability a year or more in advance of the divorce," he told me. "When they know divorce is on the horizon, business owners draw less income because they control their own compensation and simultaneously clamp down on personal spending to appear broke. Some even sell their luxury cars and buy compact cars. Others move out of the house and into a friend's guest house and never go out in public, even normal social commitments. I've seen this acting job work."

» **He doesn't take a paycheck. Everything belongs to the business.**

If your husband's business pays for his personal

expenses and belongings, then he doesn't need a paycheck, as such—and without one, he can claim he has "no income." Another advantage, from his perspective, is that in shelling out for his expenses, the business appears to take a hit both in its net income and its valuation.

» **Come to think of it, the business started having trouble just when the marriage did.** Did you wonder if stress from the troubled business was contributing to your marital difficulties? Maybe it was the other way around, and the troubled marriage signaled a convenient time for the business to experience some difficulty. It could be that your husband has been hiding assets for longer than you imagined.

» **He won't turn over the financial documents your attorney asks for.** Bank and credit card statements and copies of checks are all difficult to manipulate. If your husband is trying to create a financial impression that this third party data will not support, he will likely be reluctant to give your divorce team a chance to examine his financial records. He'll want to buy time, and also, to drive up your legal bills by forcing your attorney to make repeated demands for documentation you are legally entitled to. His reasoning, of course, is that the sooner you're out of money to pay your divorce team, the sooner you'll have to settle for less than you deserve.

» **He says the business is in difficulties, but his lifestyle sure doesn't show it.**
While some crafty business owners will put on an act to support their claims of poverty, others might maintain a lavish lifestyle, and even support a new girlfriend in high style as well. Can his reported income cover everything he's spending? If not, where's the money coming from? Gifts? Sale of marital assets? Surely it would be hard to get a bank loan, if the business were suffering as badly as he says. If something doesn't add up, the difference might be found in unreported income.

» **He pays for everything in cash now, though he always used to use a credit card to get the bonus points.**
An obvious advantage of using cash is that it so easily goes undocumented. A newfound enthusiasm for cash transactions can be a clue that all is not as it's represented to be.

It can be difficult to prove that your husband is underreporting income or misrepresenting the value of his business, especially if he controls all the financial information. Your goal is to create a credibility issue for his claims, by proving that the financial picture he's presenting the court is inconsistent with available documentation.

An entire sub-specialty of accounting, called forensic accountancy, has developed to tackle exactly this kind of problem. A forensic accountant is specifically trained to detect inconsistencies, find evidence for wrongdoing, if any, and get at the truth of a financial situation. He or she will examine every kind of business financial record in minute detail, to piece together a true financial picture. Expert help of this kind is exactly what you need to cure a case of Sudden Income Deficit Syndrome.

"The only way to catch these types of scams is to sweat the details," Attorney Mason concluded. "The tax returns must be analyzed over time—both personal and business. Have a forensic accountant look at the business's financials and loan applications and compare them to the tax returns."

Reminder: Your best defense against a case of SIDS is financial awareness. If you have a working knowledge of your husband's business income, expenses, assets, and debts, you'll sense early on whether he's underreporting his income, and you'll know where to look for cash flows he might neglect to mention.

Hot tip: Although owning a business creates numerous opportunities to do so, it is not necessary to be a business owner to underrepresent income. In other words, don't make the mistake of thinking your husband is not in a profession that affords much of a chance to squirrel away undeclared cash. The opportunity for undocumented or on-the-side work exists in nearly every job.

Legal matters: When your husband signs a Financial Affidavit, he is swearing under penalty of perjury that he has told the truth about his finances and disclosing all income, expenses, assets and liabilities. Penalties for lying under oath vary from state to state and case to case, and courts have a variety of remedies for such conduct. If your husband is found not to have told the complete truth about his finances, a judge could order him to pay your attorney fees and/or a hefty fine, or even dismiss his claims outright. In the most serious cases, he could face incarceration, if he is in contempt of court.

CHAPTER 25

WHAT CAN HAPPEN IF YOUR HUSBAND LIES ABOUT HIS FINANCES?

According to the National Endowment for Financial Education, about one-third (31 percent) of U.S. adults who combined assets with a spouse or partner admit they have been deceptive about money. What's more, women (65 percent) are more likely than men (47 percent) to say their partner or spouse lied to them about finances, debt and money earned.

As the NEFE reported in 2011[1], the study also found that:

- » Nearly three in five of those surveyed (58 percent) said they hid cash from their partner or spouse.
- » More than half (54 percent) hid a minor purchase from their partner or spouse.
- » An additional 30 percent hid a statement or a bill from their partner or spouse.

» 34 percent admitted they lied about finances, debt, money earned.

Do you suspect your husband is hiding assets? Is he being less than forthright about financial matters?

As I'm sure your divorce attorney has explained to you, each spouse is legally required to openly and honestly disclose his/her finances, including all income, expenses and debt. Unfortunately, though, it seems some people simply can't resist the temptation to lie or cheat in order to keep at least a portion of those assets solely to themselves—and it happens much more often than most women realize.

Over the years, I've seen men use a wide range of dirty tricks so they can:

» Hide, understate, or undervalue certain marital property
» Overstate debts
» Report lower than actual income
» Report higher than actual expenses

What does a husband who cheats like this hope to gain? Ultimately, a husband who is hiding assets is hoping to keep more marital property for himself while preventing his wife from getting the fair settlement she's entitled to. It's a strategy that's misguided, underhanded, deplorable . . . and completely illegal.

So, what can happen if your husband does lie about financial matters?

Plenty.

The rules of civil procedure[2] ensure that when someone signs a court document he/she is agreeing that the contents of the document are true and correct to the best of his/her knowledge and belief.

In other words, when your husband signs the Financial Affidavit[3], which is required in every contested (and even in some uncontested) divorces—he is swearing, under penalty of perjury, he is telling the truth about his finances and disclosing all assets, liabilities, income and expenses. (Yes, that means he must disclose the stock options he was granted by his employer *even if* no one specifically asked him if he had stock options.)

If your husband lies under oath, he can face very serious consequences.

Naturally, penalties vary from state to state (and from case to case), but in general terms, the law empowers the courts with a variety of different remedies for such blatant contempt of court. For instance, if your husband knowingly violates asset disclosure laws, a judge could order him to pay your attorney fees and/or fines. Or, he could be subject to a dismissal of his claims. In the most serious cases, your husband could even face incarceration.

Here's a court case that really drives home the point. Back in 1999, a Los Angeles family court judge ruled that a woman had violated state asset disclosure laws because she neglected to reveal she had won $1.3 million in the California state lottery . . . just 11 days before she filed for divorce!

According to the *Los Angeles Times*[4], the judge in this case determined that the wife had acted out of fraud or malice, and as a result, he awarded all of the winnings to the ex-husband.

Since California is a Community Property State[5], the husband would have been entitled to receive half of the lottery fortune—*if* the wife had properly disclosed it. Instead, he was awarded every penny of the $1.3 million.

If you suspect your husband could be guilty of hiding assets, please *Think Financially, Not Emotionally*[®6]. Alert your divorce team to your concerns, so you can work together to ensure you receive an equitable divorce settlement agreement.

Reminder: Lying during divorce proceedings is illegal. It's illegal for your husband, and it's illegal for you, too.

Hot tip: A Lifestyle Analysis[7] prepared by a qualified divorce financial advisor[8] can help determine if your husband is lying and/or hiding assets. As I discuss in Chapter 14, a Lifestyle Analysis identifies spending habits and day-to-day living expenses incurred during the marriage, with an emphasis on the last three to five years. Since it includes recurring and ordinary expenses, as well as unusual and non-recurring expenses, a Lifestyle Analysis can shine a spotlight on figures that "don't quite add up." That's why this type of analysis is often required by the judge as verification of the net worth and income and expense statements submitted by both spouses.

Legal matters: If it's determined that your husband cheated during your divorce proceedings, your divorce settlement agreement can be reconsidered—even after it's finalized. In a landmark case described at DivorceNet.com[9], a husband in Michigan deliberately hid assets during his divorce's primary trial period. After the divorce was finalized, the assets were uncovered. The court reconsidered the property division and eventually awarded the wife all of the found assets. (Note: Despite this positive outcome, I maintain it would have been optimal for the wife to have discovered the hidden assets during the divorce proceedings.)

CHAPTER 26

HOW TO PROTECT INHERITANCES AND GIFTS IN DIVORCE

In divorce, you'll find that every detail of your marital finances is examined very closely indeed. Your professional divorce team[1] will go through everything with a very fine-toothed comb, and your husband's team will do the same, as each of you wants to emerge from the divorce in the best possible financial shape. Each asset and debt will be identified, valued, and evaluated as to its disposition in the settlement agreement.

Some assets may have been left to you, or given as gifts, by loved ones who intended them to be for you alone, and naturally, it's important that your husband have no claim to these in your divorce. The very idea of your husband walking away with money left to you by a beloved grandparent he didn't even care about, for example, could be deeply upsetting. But is that something that might happen?

Let's take a look at this issue by reviewing the basics of asset distribution.

Whether or not a particular asset can be divided as part of a divorce settlement typically depends on how it is classified, legally. Is it considered separate property or marital property[2]?

In case you haven't read Chapter 15, let me take a minute to explain that generally speaking, in most states, **separate property** is defined as:

» property owned by either spouse before the marriage or obtained by either spouse after the Date of Separation,

» inheritances received by either spouse,

» gifts to either spouse from a third party,

» payments for pain and suffering in personal injury suits and

» property designated as separate property in a prenuptial or postnuptial agreement, if any.

(Note: Some states, such as Connecticut, Massachusetts, Michigan, and Vermont, do not typically distinguish between marital and separate property.)

All else is considered **marital property**, and how that gets divided in divorce depends on whether you live in a "Community Property" State or an "Equitable Distribution" State.

In a **Community Property State**, spouses are considered equal owners of all marital property, and assets are split 50-50. But most states (all but nine) are **Equitable Distribution States,** in which the division of marital assets is more complicated. No matter which of them is listed as the owner of a given asset, each spouse has a legal claim to a fair and equitable portion of its value. Remember that "fair and equitable" doesn't necessarily mean "half." The court considers many factors to determine what constitutes a fair and equitable distribution of marital property.

You probably noticed that inheritances and gifts to either spouse are specifically listed as assets considered to be separate property. Couldn't be simpler, right?

Well, as with many things in divorce, there are complicating factors. Here is the most crucial thing to know:

Inheritances and gifts might not be considered separate property *if they have been commingled with marital assets.*

In short, you need to actively keep your separate property separate.

If you have inherited funds or gifts intended only for you, keep that money in a separate account, in your name only. Provided you keep the money separate, and keep the separation total (do not deposit marital funds into this account), then your husband should have no claim to it.

If, however, you add marital funds to the separate account, or use the gift/inheritance toward a purchase in both your names, then at that time, the money or purchased asset may convert into marital property. ("Transmute" is the legal term for the conversion from separate to marital property.) As such, it could be subject to division in divorce.

There are additional measures to take to maintain the separation of gifted monies. Frequently, in divorce settlement negotiations, there arises a disagreement and/or muddled recollection as to whether a gift was actually a loan, or vice versa, or if it was a gift to both parties and not just to you. I've seen it happen that a gift made early in the marriage is suddenly deemed to have been a loan that needs to be paid back . . . and therefore can't be divided as part of the settlement. I've also seen cases where husbands lie and say they were intended recipients of gifts. Sadly, disingenuous claims are all too common, and they can become quite problematic. Do you really want to have to ask 95-year-old Aunt Molly to testify? What happens if she is deceased?

Divorce lawyers and financial professionals can generally make a case for whether such funds are rightly considered separate or marital property. However, you can save time, legal expense, and unpleasantness, while also avoiding the possibility of being wronged, by maintaining documentation about any such gifts or loans. If you receive or make a loan during your marriage, make sure its terms are fully documented in a written and signed promissory note. If you receive or make a gift, draw up simple paperwork indicating to whom the gift has been made, and that there is no expectation of repayment.

Though it may seem like it should go without saying that your husband would have no claim to an inheritance or gift made to you alone, you now know it isn't as simple as that. Under no circumstances should you ever deposit such funds in any joint account, use them for any joint purchase with your husband or commingle them with marital assets in any way, unless you specifically intend to make those funds marital. When in doubt, a consultation with a divorce financial professional can ensure you keep those funds in the event of a break-up.

Reminder: Divorce can bring out the worst in people, and some husbands make financial threats about keeping inheritances or gifts meant for their wives. Your best defenses against this are accurate information (know what the laws are in your state) and clear documentation (maintain paperwork concerning the nature of all gifts and loans).

Hot tip: In maintaining the separateness of inheritances and/or gifts from marital assets, it can be helpful not only to have a dedicated account in your name only, but also to use an entirely different bank from the ones at which you and your husband do business together. Under some circumstances, you might be tempted to transfer some of your own funds into a joint account. While this is still easily possible between banks, as well as between accounts in the same institution, an added degree of separation might serve to remind you that your original intent was not to commingle those funds at all.

Legal matters: Receiving a substantial gift or inheritance during your marriage provides an excellent opportunity to amend a prenuptial agreement[3], or to make or amend a postnup. (Please note: Once you are married, you can only amend a prenup with a postnup.) Even with your gifted or inherited funds kept meticulously separate so as not to be considered marital property, it can be helpful to have that intention emphasized by specific mention in a postnup. Do maintain that separation of funds, though. Any commingling could complicate the enforcement of your agreement.

CHAPTER 27

LITIGATE OR SETTLE? FIVE POINTS TO CONSIDER AS YOU DECIDE

Researchers estimate[1] that in America, there are about 2,400 divorces finalized per day. That statistic is calculated from U.S. census data and excludes numbers from states that didn't report (such as California, our most populous state), so a more accurate number would be even higher.

That's a lot of divorces! But people are often surprised to learn that the vast majority of them are never argued in a trial before a judge. In fact, about 95% of divorces are settled out of court.

What exactly does "settled out of court" mean? Well, if a couple wants to go that route, each spouse retains a professional divorce team[2], including a family law attorney, a divorce financial advisor, and other experts as the circumstances of the case require. (The more complicated the case, the more the need for a divorce financial advisor and other experts.) The attorneys, each working for their client's best interest within the laws of the state in which the divorce was filed, try to negotiate a settlement. Eventually, a compromise is forged to which both parties agree. The completed settlement agreement becomes effective when signed by both parties (and usually, the judge), and then filed with the court.

The duration of the negotiation process depends on the preparedness of each side, their willingness to work toward a solution and the complexity of issues to be decided. Some couples work out reasonable settlements without much fuss. Others, whether because they have complex financial portfolios or both parties are unwilling to compromise, run into obstacles, and negotiations can be protracted for months . . . or even years.

When the process becomes bogged down and/or contentious, it's tempting to tell the attorney to call it quits and bring the case before a judge. Nothing, it seems, could be worse than the constant struggle against someone who it seems will never compromise or worse, delights in stonewalling every attempt to move the process along.

Is that where you are? Is your husband refusing one offer after another, drawing out the process— possibly on purpose, for the satisfaction of driving up your legal fees? Your frustration is understandable. But trial may not be the best answer.

Here are five points to consider before telling your attorney to litigate:

1. Trials are very expensive.

I've seen plenty of cases where one spouse demands a trial only to end up spending more in legal fees than s/he would have lost by agreeing to even the least reasonable of the other spouse's proposals in the first place. Keep your focus on the outcome, no matter how the process, or your husband, manages to infuriate you. I have clients who've spent hundreds of thousands of dollars—or more!—on legal fees. Make sure you can reasonably expect the result to be worth the expense.

2. A trial will be a public, emotional grind.

Especially if you have children, think long and hard about whether your family can (or should) withstand the stress and public upheaval that a trial represents. Trials can be intensely ugly and emotionally damaging. In some cases, it's just not worth it.

3. Even if you can afford it, and you're up for the ordeal, your problem may not be best solved by litigation.

Are you and your husband just arguing about terms or does your stalemate arise from a more fundamental disagreement? For example, if you can't agree on the amount of spousal support, or the specific arrangements of shared child custody, then you may be better served by staying in negotiations, even if you have to adjust the negotiating team. But if you can't even agree that there will even be any spousal support, or if one of you is insisting on sole custody, the gulf between your points of view may be too wide to bridge in negotiation. A judge may have to decide for you.

4. **When you go to trial, you give control of your financial future to a judge.**

As long and hard as negotiations can be, you at least have some control and flexibility in that setting. In a courtroom, the judge's opinion is the only one that matters. You have no control over which judge hears your case, or what her biases or prejudices might be. Judges are held to a high standard of professional impartiality, but they're human, too! A judge might not see things your way, and the judge's decision is final (unless there are grounds for appeal—in which case, see #1 and #2, again).

5. **Your emotions should not govern a decision to go to trial.**

As with all aspects of the divorce process, it's essential to *Think Financially, Not Emotionally*®3 while you're deciding whether or not to go to court. Throwing up your hands in frustration and marching off to litigate in a huff will do you no good in the long run . . . and could more likely result in a financial disaster.

So, to litigate, or to settle—how should you decide? Here's a purely financial approach: Ask your attorney for her best estimate of the cost of a trial. To be safe, increase that amount by, say, one-third. Then list the dollar value of the assets or issues over which you and your husband have reached an impasse in negotiations. Set your feelings aside, and look at the numbers. Where do you stand to benefit most, in court or out?

Reminder: It bears repeating—do not make the decision to bring your case before a judge out of frustration, anger, spite or any emotion at all. If you do choose to litigate, it should be because your case is presenting difficulties that only a judge can favorably resolve.

Hot tip: If your husband refuses to disclose income and/or assets that you believe to exist, then you may need those issues to be addressed directly by a judge. Hiding assets, or failing to make full disclosure on Financial Affidavits[4] or other court documents, is illegal, and there may be very little point in negotiating with someone who is willing to use such underhanded tactics.

Legal matters: You might imagine that if your case is assigned to a female judge, she is more likely to see things your way. However, particularly if you are a stay-at-home mom[5] seeking alimony, some female judges may actually be biased *against* you. To get to the bench, she's likely had to work long, hard hours with her own children in day care. That won't make her sympathetic toward an educated, competent woman who chose to give up her career and now seeks spousal support rather than return to paid work. (I discuss more about how being a stay-at-home mom can affect your future finances in Chapter 31.)

CHAPTER 28

CHILD SUPPORT AND ALIMONY: ONCE GRANTED, MAKE SURE YOU ACTUALLY RECEIVE IT

Being awarded alimony and/or child support as part of a divorce settlement agreement can feel like a successful outcome. You may have the urge to give "high fives" all around as you breathe a huge sigh of relief that you and your children will be taken care of via regular checks from your ex. After all, he's been legally ordered to provide for you.

The sad truth of the matter, well-known by family lawyers and borne out by U.S. Census data, is that the majority of ex-husbands simply don't honor the financial terms of their divorce settlements. Many women find that even if things go well at first, eventually their checks don't come on time, don't represent the full amount owed, and/or stop coming altogether. This loss of income can result in real, significant hardship for mothers and children, not to mention the untold frustration (and expense) of seemingly endless, ineffective legal wrangling to attempt enforcement.

Is there anything you can do to avoid all that? Here's my advice for 1) during the divorce process—to help ensure you aren't chasing down support payments in the future, and 2) afterwards—if your ex is not following through with the payments he's legally obligated to make.

Don't agree to traditional alimony payments in the first place.

There are alternatives to traditional monthly alimony payments, and you should carefully consider each one. In my work as a Divorce Financial Strategist™[1] representing exclusively women, I've come to believe that if:

1. you and your spouse are working towards a negotiated settlement, and
2. there are sufficient funds available, then

an up-front, lump sum payment in lieu of alimony[2] is almost always the preferred option.

Keep detailed records. If you can't prove it's owed, you can't collect it.

Marilyn B. Chinitz[3], Esq., Partner at Blank Rome, is of one of New York's top divorce attorneys. Knowing that attempts to collect support payment arrearages often fail due to incomplete documentation, she instructs her clients to keep meticulous records concerning their support payments.

Women who can provide clear and specific evidence of arrears owed can take advantage of numerous enforcement remedies (described further below). "In real estate it's 'location, location, location.' In support collection, it's 'records, records, records,'" Attorney Chinitz told me.

Here are a few of her specific suggestions:

» As part of your settlement, have your spouse sign an authorization permitting you to obtain his future credit reports.

» Keep receipts of the items that your spouse is obligated to pay for, along with proof of any payments you made for which you are entitled to obtain reimbursement.

» Maintain records of when you receive the support payment and the exact amount you received.

» You may have to become your own private investigator. Use the internet to uncover information about your ex-husband's current lifestyle. Is he discussing recent acquisitions, travel, etc. on Facebook or other social media networks? You may find that he just acquired a new house or boat and is using your support payments to pay for his new acquisitions.

Pursue every government remedy available for recovering delinquent child support.

Under Title IV-D of the Social Security Act of 1975[4], each U.S. state and territory must have an Office of Child Support Enforcement. When notified that an ex is failing to make child support payments, these agencies can take a variety of actions to correct the situation and recover the support that is legally due. For instance, the state can:

» **Garnish wages.** The state can take money directly from the non-payor's paycheck.

» **Intercept certain funds.** The state can withhold funds, such as tax refunds, unemployment insurance payments and workers' compensation payments.

» **Place a lien on vehicles or real estate owned by the non-payor.**

» **Administer a writ or execution.** The non-payor's property can be seized and sold to help make up for the delinquent payments.

» **Suspend a passport or certain licenses.** The non-payor's passport and his driver's license, professional license, recreational licenses, etc. can all be suspended.

» **Notify credit bureaus.** Delinquent child support can be viewed as unpaid debt and so, it can negatively affect the non-payor's credit score.

» **Prosecute criminally.** Under certain circumstances, the non-payor can be criminally charged and potentially face jail time and fines.

If it's alimony you are owed, go to court to get it.

Government agencies in place to help recover delinquent child support payments do not deal with alimony. Recovering alimony payments requires going to court.

When you prove your case, a judge can order similar actions against an ex-husband who fails to pay alimony as the state can against one who fails to pay child support. Wages can be garnished, licenses suspended, etc., and although the specific consequences vary from state to state, failing to pay alimony as outlined in a divorce agreement is almost *always* considered contempt of court. Disobeying a court order is a very serious offense, punishable by fines and/or jail time.

Consider using a QDRO as a support payment enforcement tool.

As I'll discuss in the next chapter, a Qualified Domestic Relations Order (QDRO) is a court order typically used in divorce to direct the division of a spouse's retirement plan benefits[5]. Federal law provides that a retirement plan can also be used to provide child support and alimony payments. QDROs have become an increasingly important tool for collection of past due support payments, and even for securing future payments, as courts in more and more states sanction their use[6] for that purpose.

Careful review of the retirement plan by a qualified attorney is essential before drafting a QDRO to use plan funds to pay support arrearages. The plan may be restricted in whether it can pay lump sums or only distributions over time. If immediate payments are not possible, calculations must be made of the necessary value of future payments. The legal cost of drafting and reviewing the QDRO and collecting the payments should also be addressed in the QDRO.

Even with all its complexities and cautions, attorneys agree that the QDRO shows definite promise[7] as a support payment collection mechanism.

The unfortunate bottom line, as many family lawyers can tell you, is that despite available remedies, it can be very difficult to get a non-compliant ex-husband to pay up. After a long, contentious divorce, it is absolutely wretched to once again battle your ex-husband because he's ignoring his financial obligation to you and your children. With the expert help of a qualified divorce team[8], it's much less likely you'll find yourself in that situation.

Reminder: An award of child support and/or alimony does not necessarily guarantee a successful ending to your divorce. In many cases, it's the beginning of a long road of chasing down payments. To minimize legal wrangling and financial hardship, build as many safeguards and assurances into your divorce settlement agreement as you possibly can.

Hot tip: Choosing an upfront lump sum in lieu of traditional alimony payments can be the smartest way to get alimony. However, it takes exceptionally careful, disciplined, and deliberate financial management to ensure that your lump sum actually lasts as long as it's intended to. A qualified divorce financial advisor can help you design a plan that gives you solid financial footing both now and in the future.

Legal matters: If your divorce team pursues support payments through a QDRO, they will need to carefully consider the tax law involved. Retirement plans are often funded with pre-tax dollars, and payments from them can be required to be reported as income. However, the federal tax code specifically states that child support is not taxable as income to the custodial parent. Be sure that the QDRO specifies what the purpose of the payment is, and that the amount you receive is made "net" of taxes.

CHAPTER 29

USING A QDRO TO ENFORCE THE FINANCIAL TERMS OF YOUR DIVORCE SETTLEMENT

After the stress, grief and turmoil of a divorce, the last thing you want down the road is to run into difficulty getting your ex-husband to honor the financial terms of your divorce settlement. Nobody wants to be in that situation, but here's the sad truth: The majority of ex-husbands just don't honor their financial obligations set forth in their settlement agreements.

All too often, I've seen how difficult it can be to get delinquent ex-husbands to pay up. To say it's frustrating is an understatement . . . and as I discussed in the previous chapter, when child support payments are involved, well, it can be heartbreaking.

Fortunately, the Qualified Domestic Relations Order (QDRO) is emerging as an effective mechanism to ensure that divorced women actually receive the support payments their ex-husbands have been legally ordered to make. Here's what you need to know about QDROs, and what they can be used for. Let's start at the beginning . . .

What exactly is a Qualified Domestic Relations Order?

In legal terms, a Qualified Domestic Relations Order (QDRO)[1] is a judgment, decree or order that creates or recognizes the existence of an alternate payee's right to receive, or assigns to an alternate payee the right to receive, all or a portion of the benefits payable to a participant in a retirement plan.

QDROs are typically used in divorce settlement agreements to ensure equitable division of a spouse's retirement plan benefits[2]. A judge can use a QDRO to order that you receive part of your husband's retirement benefits, including pension plans, 401(k) s, 403(b)s, and other Employee Retirement Income Security Act (ERISA)[3]-governed plans (but, notably, not IRAs).

Federal law allows retirement plans also to be used as a source of funds for child support and alimony payments. With this in mind, divorce attorneys are increasingly finding that a QDRO has uses beyond serving as part of a divorcing woman's financial strategy for retirement. It can also be an excellent tool for ensuring or collateralizing payment of spousal or child support as ordered in the divorce settlement.

Matt Lundy[4], Esq., an attorney with specific expertise in QDROs, told me that QDROs have become an extremely effective tool in eliminating the "middle man" (i.e., an obstinate opposing party) in obtaining monies from an ERISA-based retirement account.

"Very few attorneys have any understanding as to what a QDRO is and how it may be used, but with the right wording, and a general understanding of the law and the dynamics of the Plan, a QDRO could be a tremendous tool to ensure fairness," he explained.

Beyond splitting retirement plan savings, what can a QDRO do for you in divorce?

Your husband's retirement plan funds can legally be accessed for several purposes. Here are four things your divorce team can use a QDRO to do for you:

1. **Secure temporary support.**

    A QDRO can be used to ensure temporary support payments while your case is pending. For instance, a judge can order an interim award of Equitable Distribution via a QDRO, so that a woman without access to sufficient cash can retain a professional divorce team[5].

2. **Collect attorney's fees.**

    ERISA[6] specifies that QDROs must relate to support or property division, but that doesn't mean they can't be used to collect your attorney's fees. Many courts recognize that attorney's fees qualify fairly as support, because without an attorney, you would not be able to proceed with your divorce on equal footing with your husband.

According to Attorney Lundy, QDROs can be particularly effective for collection of delinquent temporary support and/or temporary attorney's fees.

"In the event that you have an order of contempt entered against an opposing party for the failure to pay temporary support or temporary attorney's fees, consider asking the judge to reserve jurisdiction to subsequently enter a QDRO, if it becomes necessary to effectuate the original temporary relief order," he said. "A QDRO and similar orders will eliminate any reliance on an unwilling opposing party to satisfy his/her obligation by taking the chips right out of their hand and getting direct payment from the retirement plan. Of course, it is always in your best interest to retain an experienced QDRO attorney to streamline this process."

3. **Collateralize alimony and other support.**
A judge can order that if your husband does not pay alimony, child support, or other post-divorce financial obligations through the means agreed to in your settlement agreement, these

funds can be taken directly from his retirement plan. This is using a QDRO essentially as a lien on your husband's retirement accounts. (Again, this applies only to ERISA[7]-governed accounts such as pension plans and 401(k)s, and *not* to IRAs and the like.)

How does this work? Usually, the divorce settlement agreement would specify a certain dollar amount or percentage of the retirement plan to be assigned via QDRO to you, the recipient spouse, as part of equitable distribution. The remaining share would stay "as is," for your ex-husband. The settlement agreement would also provide you, via QDRO, with a security interest—the "lien"—in this remaining share, to secure his obligation to you.

4. Recover delinquent support payments.

If your ex never makes the payments he's agreed to, or if the checks stop coming, it can be exceedingly difficult to recover what you are owed. A QDRO can help. Support arrearages can be ordered to be paid through your non-paying ex's retirement plan.

This definitely requires expert professional help. Meticulous review by a qualified attorney is essential. Retirement plans have various restrictions as to whether payments can be made by lump sum, or only in distributions over time. Immediate payments may not be legally possible, and calculations will need to be made of the necessary value of future payments.

Of course, it is always better to lay the groundwork against this situation before your divorce is final.

"Even if you are pursuing a retirement asset only to secure payment of alimony or child support rather than claiming part of it in your property distribution, it's best to take care of the QDRO requirements during the divorce or simultaneously with the divorce judgment, because you may not be able to go back and do it later," cautions Bari Z. Weinberger[8], Esq., owner and managing partner of the Weinberger Law Group, a firm exclusively devoted to family law in New Jersey. "In New Jersey, if the retirement plan is 'qualified' under ERISA, then it can be divided as an asset or used for child support or alimony. In addition, if you have a pension that falls under the New Jersey State-administered retirement system, The NJ Division of Pensions and Benefits will honor court orders for child support, alimony, or equitable distribution."

Reminder: It is always best to think ahead, and think protectively. Your husband may show every sign of honoring his post-divorce financial obligations to you, but many divorced women and divorce professionals can tell you that more often than not, this changes—and you and your children would bear the consequences. If you are negotiating a divorce settlement, including a QDRO to collateralize support payments is much preferable to drafting one later to recover arrearages.

Hot tip: QDROs are complicated to prepare, and many attorneys outsource them to specialists within the field. Make sure that the cost of drafting and reviewing the QDRO, and collecting the payments it orders, is itself addressed in the QDRO.

Legal matters: In pursuing support payments through a QDRO, tax law should be carefully considered. Retirement plans are often funded with pre-tax dollars, and payments from them can be considered taxable income (though you may be able to avoid the withholding tax if you transfer those funds directly into an IRA). However, the federal tax code specifically states that child support is *not* taxable as income to the custodial parent. Be sure that your QDRO specifies what the purpose of the payment is, and that the amount you receive is made "net" of taxes.

CHAPTER 30

HOW ALIMONY "REFORM" MIGHT AFFECT YOU NOW AND IN THE FUTURE

In recent years, several state legislatures have focused their attention on so-called alimony reform. Sponsors and supporters of these proposed new laws claim that traditional alimony is obsolete because many of the laws on the books today were enacted in a time when most marriages lasted for decades and women did not work outside the home. Back then, if it were not for alimony, divorce would leave former wives without any means of financial support. Since none of that is true in today's society, would-be alimony reformers argue that changes are long overdue.

I agree that social and economic circumstances have substantially changed the way we approach marriage, divorce and divorce settlements. And certainly, more women are financially independent today than ever before. However, it is still true that many divorcing women can't immediately generate sufficient income to support themselves, let alone maintain anything close to their marital lifestyle. Clearly, alimony still has a role to play in the fair settlement of divorce, even if alimony laws are adjusted to reflect modern realities.

Let's back up a bit, and review some **alimony basics**:

Simply stated, alimony is *court-ordered payment from one former spouse to the other after divorce.* Alimony can be mutually agreed upon pursuant to a divorce settlement agreement, and it's intended for the financial support of the spouse who was financially dependent during the marriage—even today, this is still usually the wife. In general, alimony is paid in one of three ways: 1) as a lump sum[1], 2) in regular payments without a fixed end date ("permanent alimony"), or 3) according to some interim arrangement ("temporary" or "rehabilitative" alimony).

The amount and duration of alimony is decided according to applicable laws in each state, which vary widely. In most states, judges have significant discretion to evaluate the circumstances of individual cases.

Most alimony reform measures attempt to limit or remove this judicial discretion and impose severe limitations on what can be awarded in any given case. (Usually, if a judge deviates from the specifications of these new laws, s/he is required to give a detailed written explanation as to why. Given the caseloads these judges bear, many will simply opt to work within the new parameters.) The goals, it seems, are to eliminate permanent alimony altogether and limit the amount and duration of temporary alimony as much as possible.

New Jersey made headlines in 2014 for enacting a law that significantly restricts a judge's discretion regarding the terms of alimony that can be awarded as part of a divorce settlement agreement. In 2013, Florida's Governor Rick Scott vetoed a bill that would ban permanent alimony and impose very strict limits on temporary alimony (its advocates have promised to reintroduce the bill by eliminating the retroactive portion of the bill that Governor Scott cited as his reason for vetoing it). In 2011, Massachusetts passed legislation that ends alimony upon the payor's retirement and links duration of alimony to the length of a marriage.

What's the problem with all of that?

Having spent years helping women navigate the financial aspects of their divorces[2], I can assure you that alimony is far from obsolete. It's an essential means of financial support for many divorcing women, especially in cases in which:

» She gave up her potential career and earning power and invested her time and labor into the family.

» She managed the household, allowing her husband to invest in his career, increasing his earning power while hers languished. Many divorcing women set aside educational and employment opportunities. Many also helped (financially or otherwise) their husbands attain professional degrees or training.

» At the time of the divorce, he is often at the peak of his earning potential (thanks in no small part to his wife), while she has become relatively unemployable (except, in many cases, for low-paying clerical or entry-level jobs).

» Though they may be dividing assets 50-50, he, because of his earning power, can often replace those assets relatively quickly and continue to build wealth. She, because of her lack of earning power, most likely will be liquidating assets from day one and will ultimately go broke.

Some proposed alimony reforms make good sense. Yes, judges should be able to nix a high alimony award when circumstances plainly don't warrant it. Yes, alimony payments should be determined in part by the payor's ability to pay and the payee's need. And, yes, the term of alimony should be directly related to the length of the marriage.

However, many "reform" advocates are pushing to go well beyond these reasonable adjustments.

Laws that change alimony practices retroactively are particularly troubling. Consider, for example, a woman who gave up a house or other major assets in her divorce agreement, in favor of a certain amount of alimony for a certain period of time. In some circumstances, this can be a financially wise arrangement, and it's not uncommon. But, if a new law comes along that retroactively changes divorce settlements, this woman may find that her ex-husband can get the alimony reduced or eliminated, even though there's no way for her to get the house back, and she can't renegotiate any other aspects of the divorce agreement!

What can women do to protect themselves?

More than ever, women need to safeguard their financial futures before and during their marriages. To that end, I always advise brides-to-be[3] to communicate openly and thoroughly with their fiancés about finances, and for couples to have prenuptial agreements specifying what they will consider separate and marital property in the event of a break-up.

Postnuptial agreements are increasingly important, as well. For instance, if a couple decides that the wife will give up paid work[4] to devote her time to management and care of home and family, I think both husband and wife should sign a postnup that clearly outlines how she would be compensated, in the event of a divorce, for having given up her career. Given the current trend in alimony reform, I recommend that, if possible, this be an upfront lump sum. (I'll discuss more about how being a stay-at-home mom can impact your future finances in the next chapter.)

Stay-at-home moms and other women with little or no income of their own appear to have lost support in state legislatures largely controlled by men (many of whom might have their own alimony obligations which they resent). With alimony reform in different forms and stages around the country, today's divorcing woman must be vigilant. Know what's going on where you live, and hire divorce professionals who stay on top of the news and will adjust your strategy according to what's happening in the legislature.

Reminder: Divorcing women often hear that they can "just go back to school and find a job." But even in a healthy economy, those who've been out of the work force for decades won't find this an easy proposition. Don't be talked out of seeking alimony due to an errant notion that it will be easy or simple to re-enter the workforce.

Hot tip: If there are sufficient assets available, an upfront lump sum payment in lieu of alimony is the best option in many divorce cases. An upfront lump sum payment in lieu of alimony will bypass any complications due to alimony reform that could come your way.

Legal matters: State laws differ regarding all aspects of divorce, but there is especially wide variation in the laws governing spousal support. In some states, alimony is limited by law to only those who have been married for 10 years or longer. In others, the law says that spousal support must be permanent. Clearly, it is worth knowing what the laws are where you live; and, if you have a choice of jurisdiction and are in a position to plan, you should evaluate carefully where would be best for you to file for divorce.

SPECIAL
TOPICS

*Volume I ends with an overview of prenups, postnups,
and how to divorce-proof your business. Here, you'll
learn about other factors that can impact your divorce,
including how much you currently earn, where you have
citizenship (and/or where he does), and why you need to
Think Financially, Not Emotionally®.*

CHAPTER 31

HOW BEING A STAY-AT-HOME MOM CAN AFFECT YOUR DIVORCE AND YOUR FUTURE FINANCES

Many are surprised when I mention this, but according to the latest statistics from the U.S. Department of Labor, women still comprise less than half of the total U.S. workforce (46.9% in 2012) . . . and where child-rearing is concerned, you don't even need to consult official figures—just take a look at any elementary school during weekday morning drop-off. Chances are, you'll see many more Mommies than Daddies. Why? Because the reality is that it's still usually the wife who becomes the stay-at-home parent.

As a husband and a father, I realize "opting out" of the paid workforce to care for your children can be tremendously fulfilling, and I know that many women wouldn't want it any other way.

However, as a Divorce Financial Strategist™[1], it's my job to remind you that you need to realize that opting to become a stay-at-home mom (SAHM) is a choice that all but ensures a significant financial loss.

Let me explain.

If you're like many women, your story goes something like this:

You went to school, earned your degree(s), and launched a career that you're proud of. Things moved along pretty well, thanks to your hard work, long hours, and commitment, and you established an excellent professional reputation and a comfortable salary.

Your husband's experiences have been quite similar. Maybe the two of you met in college, or as young professionals. As you fell in love and married, both of your careers gained traction and both salaries followed suit. Over time, you began thinking about starting a family . . .

And here's where your story begins to take a significantly different turn from your husband's.

If you decide to become a SAHM, it's unlikely you'll recover that kind of career momentum *or* earning potential. Plus, the longer you're out of the job market, the more difficult it will be to get back in.

To be sure, in my line of work, I don't meet many "happily ever after" SAHMs. In fact, many of the women who consult with me are facing life as a jobless single mother, and they need help navigating the divorce process to their best possible financial advantage.

Why? Because the legal and financial picture for a divorcing SAHM can be quite complicated. For instance, if you're a divorcing SAHM, you should never assume that because managing house, home, and family has been your full-time occupation, you will receive alimony covering your full support. Today, family courts expect you to support yourself, and being a caretaker will not excuse you from that expectation.

"What we often find is that many stay-at-home parents, either moms or dads, as is becoming more common, go into the divorce process assuming that lifetime alimony covering full support is a given. In this day and age, however, this kind of expectation is simply not realistic," said Bari Z. Weinberger[2], Esq., owner and managing partner of the Weinberger Law Group, a firm exclusively devoted to family law in New Jersey.

As I discussed in the previous chapter, alimony reform is changing the way the legal system views requests for spousal support[3].

"In states such as Massachusetts, that have seen alimony reform laws passed in recent years, 'permanent' lifetime alimony awards are all but abolished, except under certain circumstances," Attorney Weinberger explained. "In other states, including New Jersey, permanent alimony is still available, but is far less likely to be awarded just because a parent decided to leave their career to stay home with the kids. What is becoming more the norm for stay-at-home moms and dads is 'rehabilitative' or 'temporary' alimony that's put in place to help the spouse get on their feet long enough to re-enter the workforce."

In some states, no alimony is allowed for marriages of less than a specified number of years. All others require that a woman must prove not only that she needs alimony, but also that her husband can afford to pay it!

If your state hasn't enacted one or more laws like this, don't be complacent. It's possible that there might be similar bills pending in your legislature.

As a divorcing SAHM, you'll be facing these legal realities and may be required to pursue full-time paid work immediately—while proving your efforts in detail to a skeptical court. Alternatively, the court may impute a certain income for you, whether you can realistically earn it or not, and that will effectively reduce or eliminate the amount of alimony you might receive. Many SAHMs end up taking jobs ill-suited to their education and skill sets. And while they may ultimately land on their feet, it isn't without years of hardship and struggle.

If you are, or are planning to become, a SAHM, what can you do to protect yourself?

First, check out the alimony laws in your state. And if you don't like what you find (and I'm sure you won't), make sure you have a legal agreement with your husband that protects you better than your legislature will.

In other words . . .

Prepare and sign a formal postnuptial agreement with your husband.

Everyone has heard of prenuptial agreements, or "prenups." They're legal documents, signed before marriage, and they detail what property rights and expectations would be in the event of a divorce. Correctly drafted[4], a prenup can be an excellent way to supersede your state's divorce laws, and a *postnuptial* agreement can accomplish those same goals . . . the difference is that a postnup is negotiated and signed *after* the couple is already married.

I firmly believe that prenups and postnups are good for marriages. After all, if you are about to become a stay-at-home mom, working out a postnuptial agreement provides you and your husband an excellent opportunity to talk seriously and candidly about the financial implications of the decision. Think about how your relationship with your husband might change, or has changed, with your financial dependence on him. How will you value each other's time and commitments outside the home? If the family income is "his," how does that affect how the two of you make decisions about saving, spending and investing that money?

In a postnup, you can clearly define the parameters surrounding your decision to leave your job. You can quantify what you're giving up, put it in writing and sign your names to it. This makes your financial sacrifice tangible—and makes it more difficult to minimize later (as unfortunately, I've heard husbands try to do far too often).

Working out a postnuptial agreement[5] to ensure your financial security as you leave paid work provides a great opportunity to talk with your husband about the financial implications of that decision. Don't shortchange the sacrifice you're about to make. Once you've laid out the risks—loss of income, career momentum, and earning potential are just a few— the wisdom of a postnup becomes clear (Not every state recognizes postnups, so please discuss what is allowable in your state with a divorce attorney who is highly experienced in drafting prenups and postnups). Then, with the help of that qualified attorney, you can get into the details.

A postnup should specify how you'll be supported if your marriage ends. (Given the current trend in alimony reform, I recommend, if possible, this be an upfront lump sum amount in lieu of monthly payments of alimony.) It can also stipulate how long you expect to be out of work. (And of course, you can amend it in future, if need be.)

When they first consult with me, my clients are beginning to experience the clarity of hindsight. By the time their divorces and settlement agreements are finalized, they've realized there are things they would have done very differently in their marriages, financially speaking.

"If a couple never executed a prenuptial agreement, or does have one, but it doesn't address spousal support, it can feel like you've missed the boat," Attorney Weinberger concluded. "Thanks to postnuptial agreements, you still have time to establish provisions to protect you financially should you make that leap to stay home and raise your kids."

You already know that agreeing to be the "at-home" Mom, while certainly rewarding, will also be a sacrifice on many levels. Please remember that much of this sacrifice is financial, and that you, not your husband, will be taking the brunt of it. Just as having a prenup is an essential component of my financial advice for brides-to-be[6], I consider a postnuptial agreement critical to your financial security as a stay-at-home mom.

Reminder: While you are by no means agreeing to an employer/employee relationship with your husband, you should think of the postnup in a similarly businesslike way: You are entering a new work situation, and it is reasonable and wise to set forth conditions for your financial security as you do so.

Hot tip: If you will be out of your profession for a significant time, you might want to consult with a vocational expert[7] to discuss ways of keeping your skills and contacts current. Ask for leads on part time work that can keep you "opted-in" without shortchanging your time with your children.

Legal matters: While you might think that drawing a female judge for your case puts you at an advantage, the opposite can actually be true. Think about it: Many female judges likely had their own kids in day care while pursing demanding legal careers. Why would they be more empathetic toward an educated, capable woman who willingly gave up her earning potential?

CHAPTER 32

SPECIAL CONSIDERATIONS FOR DIVORCING WOMEN WHO EARN MORE THAN THEIR HUSBANDS

These days, it's not uncommon for a wife's income to exceed her husband's. Sure, it's far from typical—in fact, according to a 2013 study[1], the wife's income was greater than the husband's in only 16 percent of the dual-income households surveyed—but it isn't exactly unheard of anymore, either.

If you're a woman who earns more than her husband or one who owns greater personal assets than he does, you owe it to yourself to pay close attention to certain financial matters that are relevant throughout your relationship—before you say "I do," during the marriage and then later, if you decide to divorce. For instance, it's essential for you to:

Have clear legal agreements, including a prenuptial agreement, about who owns what.

A prenuptial agreement[2] is generally drawn up to protect the spouse with greater assets from losing an unfair proportion of those assets in case of a divorce. It used to be considered somewhat insulting to ask for one; however, these days, prenups are increasingly recognized to be reasonable, thoughtful formalizations of agreements between spouses-to-be as to what assets will be considered marital property and what will be maintained as separate property.

As Bari Z. Weinberger[3], Esq., owner and managing partner of the Weinberger Law Group, a firm exclusively devoted to family law in New Jersey, told me, most of her clients recognize the prenup as an intelligent business plan so that in the event of a divorce, the couple can save significant funds in lieu of litigating these issues.

"Naturally, the couple appreciates that the financial resources saved by avoiding litigation can be better applied toward child related expenses or future retirement funding," Attorney Weinberger said.

Keep some of your money separate.

I advise all women, whether or not divorce seems to be on the horizon, to keep a bank account of their own, one that their husband can't access and, maybe, that he doesn't even know about. This is a sure way to maintain some control over your financial independence, even as a married woman. Whether or not you tell your husband about this[4] is entirely up to you. Every marriage is different, and while some husbands encourage the separation of funds, others may be outraged. (See Chapter 2 for more a more in-depth discussion about keeping a secret fund.)

Maintain inheritance assets separately.

Attorney Weinberger pointed out that in order to secure exemption status on inheritance assets, the receiving party must maintain the assets separately.

"Do not put the other spouse's name on the asset or accounts. Do not commingle the assets or funds with marital assets or funds. Do not utilize the inheritance monies for marital purposes, such as to pay off an existing mortgage on the marital home (unless it is specifically designated in a formal, written mid-marriage agreement to enjoy on-going exemption status)," she advised. "If you do, you run the risk that the entire remainder of the inheritance will change nature and become subject to division with your spouse upon divorce, even if the grantor never intended for it to be shared."

Safeguard your business.

If you own your own business or professional partnership, this doubtless represents years of education, long hours of hard work and untold sacrifice of many kinds. You've earned your position, and you don't want to see these hard-won gains put at risk in the event of a divorce.

There are several established types of trusts and agreements that can help. The laws that govern them vary from state to state and can change often. You'll need current, expert professional advice to determine what's right for you. Even if you're single or happily married, it's wise to hire a divorce financial advisor to help you evaluate the best financial options available to divorce-proof your business[5].

Reminder: No matter what the earning differential between you and your husband, it always makes sense to follow these fundamental steps: Communicate clearly and often about finances. Take practical and legal measures to maintain your independence. Safeguard your business. Control your own circumstances. And, as always, *Think Financially, Not Emotionally*[®6] when it comes to managing your money and planning for a secure financial future.

Hot tip: Spousal abuse occurs in all socio-economic groups and between spouses of all ages and incomes, so clearly, earning more does not make you immune to domestic violence. If you're the top wage earner in your relationship, some people might assume you're somehow immune to being physically or emotionally abused. Sadly, though, that's not the case. If you are suffering spousal abuse, don't let your larger income contribute to a feeling of shame. Get help[7].

Legal matters: If you are already married, it's too late to draw up a prenup. However, married couples can draw up agreements called "postnups," and although they are not as bullet-proof as prenups, they are better than nothing at all. Let me add one important caveat here: Many states don't recognize postnuptial agreements, and even in those that do, they are frequently challenged and can be invalidated.

As I see it, though, the larger goal still stands. It's vitally important to maintain crystal clear lines of communication about these financial issues with your husband, and to formalize your agreements when possible. Treat it as a sign of mutual respect in the marriage, and esteem for your own worth, as well. Then, if the marriage does end in divorce, you will have done yourself a huge favor by having agreements in place.

CHAPTER 33

WHAT WOMEN NEED TO KNOW ABOUT DUAL CITIZENSHIP AND DIVORCE

We live in a global society fueled by a global economy, and thanks to the internet, it's easier than ever for people to stay in touch across international boundaries. As a result, marriages involving spouses from different countries are now quite common—which only means, of course, that divorces involving dual citizenship are becoming increasingly common, as well.

If you are a woman who is part of mixed-citizenship marriage and you are contemplating divorce while you're living overseas, you need to understand that divorces involving dual citizenship(s) are notoriously complex. Here are a few of the most important things you need to know:

The U.S. Department of State acknowledges that a person can be a citizen of two countries at the same time.

From the U.S. Department of State website:

A U.S. citizen may acquire foreign citizenship by marriage, or a person naturalized as a U.S. citizen may not lose the citizenship of the country of birth. U.S. law does not mention dual nationality or require a person to choose one citizenship or another. Also, a person who is automatically granted another citizenship does not risk losing U.S. citizenship. However, a person who acquires a foreign citizenship by applying for it may lose U.S. citizenship. In order to lose U.S. citizenship, the law requires that the person must apply for the foreign citizenship voluntarily, by free choice, and with the intention to give up U.S. citizenship. There are laws in some other countries that may confer citizenship there automatically. For example, this can happen if a child is born to American citizens in another country, or through marriage, or if a person does not lose the citizenship of the country of her birth on becoming a naturalized U.S. citizen.

Dual nationals owe allegiance to two countries and are required to obey the laws of both.

If your husband has dual citizenship (or "dual nationality," as it's also called), and you're living abroad, the court with jurisdiction over your divorce will most likely be the one in the country where you live—even if you're a U.S. citizen.

Are you thinking about divorcing overseas? If so, where you are residing can have an enormous impact on how your case will be resolved.

As we all know, countries vary in their legal views of women's rights, acceptable grounds for divorce, alimony, property distribution, child custody and child support, among other things. If you're living in a country that doesn't afford women the same rights as men, it could be very, very difficult to get divorced at all, let alone achieve a fair settlement.

Jeremy D. Morley[1], Esq., who is a New York lawyer and the author of *International Family Law Practice*[2] and *The Hague Abduction Convention: Practical Issues and Procedures for the Family Lawyer*[3], as well as numerous articles on international family law, summed it up nicely.

"The difference between getting divorced in London instead of in New York can be staggering," he explained.

Likewise, the disparity between the practices of divorce courts in Tokyo as compared to those in Sydney, and of the divorce courts in Hong Kong as compared to those in Frankfurt, may be equally vast—or possibly even more so.

Even though there is no treaty between the U.S. and any other country ensuring recognition of foreign divorces, divorces obtained in foreign countries are generally legally recognized here, if both parties were

living in the country in question when it was issued.

In other words, if you and your husband were both living abroad at the time of your divorce, then it's likely your divorce is legal in the U.S.

As you might expect, international family lawyers are often called upon to advise whether or not a foreign divorce will be fully recognized. Surprisingly, though, providing such advice is often difficult and sometimes fraught with risk.

"It would be reasonable to expect that legislatures and courts would have developed clear 'cut and dried' answers to as basic a question as 'Are we divorced?'" Attorney Morley said. "However, when that question is asked in the context of a foreign divorce the answer all too often is, 'It depends.'"

Please note: Several states, including California, will *not* recognize a divorce decree obtained abroad when both spouses were living in their home state. If you're unsure about the validity of a foreign divorce, you should contact the Attorney General's office in your state. You will need copies of all the documentation of your marriage, your divorce, and applicable foreign laws.

Being well-prepared, well-informed and well-advised about the divorce process is important for any woman who's going through a divorce,

**but it's especially critical for someone with an
international component to her marriage.**

Divorces involving dual citizenship are often
quite complicated. I believe *every* divorcing woman
should hire a team of qualified professionals[4] to help
navigate the divorce process—and in cases involving
dual citizenship, this kind of multi-specialty support
is even more critical. At the very least, you will need
someone on your side who is expert in the divorce
and family laws of the other country, as well as an
experienced divorce financial advisor to help you
with the financial details.

"As people travel, set up residences in different
countries, and become involved in international
business (and personal) affairs, they necessarily
expose their personal lives to an array of different
legal structures," Attorney Morley concluded. "In
some quarters, forum-shopping is a dirty term, but
in international family law it is often an essential
process. In fact, it could even be considered gross
negligence if a divorce lawyer were to select the
appropriate jurisdiction based on the location of the
lawyer's office rather than on the best interests of the
client. If the client has the option of bringing suit
in more than one jurisdiction it is absurd to suggest
that the lawyer does not have a serious obligation
to consider which jurisdiction would likely yield the
preferable result."

Reminder: As our world continues to get smaller and smaller, international and/or dual citizenship divorces are going to become increasingly common. The good news is that as these cases become more routine, more help will become available for women facing the challenges of dual-citizenship divorce.

Hot tip: If you own home(s) abroad and have flexibility as to the location and timing of your divorce, it is well worth the effort to research what the most favorable venue might be.

Legal matters: If you have children, you may want to add an expert in international custody issues to your divorce team. International custody issues are notoriously complicated, the laws are hard to enforce, and the stakes could not be higher. We've all heard horrifying news items about parental kidnapping, in which one parent takes the child(ren) to another country, and the other parent fights for years, at tremendous expense, in hopes of bringing them back to the U.S.—sometimes without success. In 2012, actress Kelly Rutherford's divorce made headlines[5] when a judge ordered her two American children to move to France because their father— who is a German citizen — was expelled from the United States.

CHAPTER 34

DIVORCE "DON'TS"

While my professional expertise is in financial matters, my business[1] has given me valuable insight into how women experience other aspects of the divorce process, as well. I've seen many success stories, as well as some settlements that were, frankly, not as favorable as they might have been.

You might be surprised to learn that some of the factors that can put a successful divorce settlement agreement at extreme risk have nothing to do with errors or omissions on financial documents.

Here are five things I've seen seriously compromise a woman's position in divorce negotiations, and I can whole-heartedly tell you that you'd be better off passing up these activities until after the ink is dry on your decree. In each case, I do recognize the temptation; but, having seen the consequences to divorcing women who've indulged in these behaviors, I strongly recommend you abstain.

Shopping (aka, Retail Therapy)

There's no question that it can feel good (in the short term, at least) to buy yourself something new when the world is getting you down. In fact, many women find that a little "retail therapy" now and then can go a long way to lift their spirits during the divorce process. But please, resist the urge to spend lavishly—or for spite. In settlement negotiations, you'll want to present yourself and your spending habits as prudent and responsible, not impulsive, and any excessive (revenge) spending *can* backfire and be viewed as dissipation of marital assets.

Dating

It can be a real joy to have someone new in your life. But truly, it's best if you don't begin any romantic relationships until you have your divorce decree in hand. Believe it or not, having an intimate relationship with someone new before you are officially divorced is legally considered adultery in some states. Don't even set up a profile on an online dating service, if you don't want it displayed in court! Dating, or even signaling your availability to date, before your divorce is final can seriously jeopardize your standing in settlement negotiations. And take note: Having "sleepovers" with someone new can affect child custody decisions.

Snooping

This can be a particularly difficult urge to resist, if you and your husband are no longer communicating directly, and you have reason to suspect he is up to no good[2]. However, if you find yourself thinking about scrolling through his text messages or emails, please think again. If you give in to this impulse, you may, in fact, run afoul of the law.

Applicable laws vary from state to state, but it is safe to assume that intentionally intercepting wire, oral, or electronic communication ("wiretapping") is illegal. Now that digital communication is the norm, privacy laws have some catching up to do. With the increase in technology in our daily lives has come an increase in sophisticated, high-tech ways to snoop into others' communications. While it is clearly illegal to install spyware on a computer owned by someone else, the law is murkier when it comes to such installation on a computer shared by spouses. I recommend that you err on the side of caution, take the high road, talk to your divorce attorney, and stay out of trouble.

Texting

I mentioned this in Chapter 8, but let me stress it again here: Every type of electronic communication has the potential to leave a digital trail, and these "trails" can be accessible and subpoenaed. That means that any of your texts, emails, etc., can end up being scrutinized by your husband's divorce team in hopes of making you look bad, and improving his case against you.

Here's an indication how common this is these days: Fully 92 percent of the nation's top divorce attorneys say they have seen an increase in the number of cases using evidence taken from smartphones over a recent three-year period, according to a survey[3] of the American Academy of Matrimonial Lawyers (AAML). In addition, nearly all (94 percent) of the respondents cited an overall rise in the use of text messages as evidence during the same time period.

Tweeting (and the like)

Social media takes the problems of texting and email and brings them to an even more dangerous level—often with pictures to raise the stakes even higher. Status updates, online photo albums, profile pages, comments, etc. can all be used as evidence to help prove infidelity, mishandling and hiding of assets, emotional instability, alcohol and drug problems, etc.

As with smartphone evidence, the AAML has also found[4] that social media sites now play a prominent role in many divorce cases. In 2014, 81 percent of AAML members cited an increase in the use of evidence from social networking websites during the past five years. Nearly two-thirds (66 percent) reported Facebook as the primary source of this type of evidence.

So, don't shop, date, snoop, text, or tweet . . . hardly seems fair, does it? Well, maybe it's not fair, but it is simple, and it is temporary. During the divorce, your conduct should be unimpeachable. You want your husband to have absolutely no cause, and no way, to cast your character in a negative light before a judge. Holding back from these activities is one way you can *Think Financially, Not Emotionally®*[5] to ensure the best possible outcome of your divorce, and the strongest possible foundation for your future.

Reminder: When I urge you not to start a new romantic relationship until you're officially single again, I'm thinking specifically of protecting yourself in the divorce process. It's also worth noting that many therapists give this same advice for psychological and emotional reasons. No matter how single you feel, there is a shift in your outlook that happens when your divorce is final and you are legally unattached. Many therapists feel that it's best to hold off on romance until you've established yourself on solid emotional ground as a single woman.

Hot tip: Here's the rule of thumb I recommend for social media: You should think of anything you tweet, say, or post on Facebook or any social media site, as if it were broadcast, in prime time, to the whole world . . . with the people most likely to use it against you sitting in the proverbial front row. For most people, that could cut down social media posting considerably.

Legal matters: Discuss privacy laws with your attorney to learn what laws apply to your emails, etc. You'll want a working knowledge of those laws, not to see what you can get away with, but to know what your rights are if you suspect your husband of spying on *you.*

CHAPTER 35

FIVE TRAITS OF WOMEN WHO COME THROUGH DIVORCE WITH DIGNITY AND A SUCCESSFUL SETTLEMENT

In my work, I have noticed over the years that some women come through the divorce process especially well. Their inner strength and dignity remain intact—or are even enhanced—and they look to the future with vigor and enthusiasm. These women don't necessarily have "easy" divorces. On the contrary, many of them have overcome abusive relationships[1] or ended marriages to narcissists[2]. What they *do* have, or find within themselves, are certain coping mechanisms and personality traits that keep them moving confidently forward through the divorce process.

Here's my short list of these traits, the ones I've observed in women who successfully survive divorce:

1. **They're able to compartmentalize and put emotions on the back burner.**

   As I tell every one of our clients, it is absolutely critical that you *Think Financially, Not Emotionally*[®3] during your divorce settlement negotiation process. Of course, that's easier said than done. Divorce is an intense personal struggle, and it's only natural that you are going to have strong emotions about it, especially concerning your children.

   Still, you must work to keep your feelings in check so you can think clearly about the important financial decisions ahead of you. Remember, these decisions have the potential to affect you for the rest of your life, and this is NOT the time to take actions out of spite or malice . . . or even sadness, for that matter. Be objective and practical, instead. It's not that you won't rant and rave, or cry until you feel you can't anymore. But there's a time and place for everything. Imagine you're putting your emotions in a box, which you can take out when you're at liberty to do so. For now, put your game face on, and *Think Financially, Not Emotionally*[®4].

2. **They ask for help and delegate tasks to appropriate people in professional and personal contexts.**

   Many of my clients would laugh when I say "divorce can be difficult"—not because it isn't true, but because it's the understatement of the century. The good news: Nobody has to go through it alone. Recognize that you will need professional and personal help and assemble the best experts[5] you can reasonably afford. Ideally, your divorce team will include professionals who can help you address not only legal issues, but also financial matters and emotional concerns, as well. Then, rally friends and family to take care of you as only those who know and love you best can. Who's a good listener? Who can always make you laugh? (If you're someone who doesn't like to ask for help . . . well, get over it. Think about what you'd do for a friend in need, and let your friends do that for you.) Get your professional and personal support networks humming . . . and use them.

3. **They get organized—and stay organized. That way, there's no unnecessary stress created by losing a document or forgetting an appointment.**

   Divorce proceedings require you to juggle many things, all at once. To keep all those balls (or maybe they feel like chainsaws!) in the air, it's imperative that you stay organized. You'll have appointments and deadlines to track—and more paperwork than you ever thought possible. There are plenty of great programs and apps out there to help you keep track of things, so this might be a good time to upgrade your technology or buy a new computer (though, unless you're very computer savvy, you may not want to switch to an entirely unfamiliar operating system). A more low-tech approach can work well, too—certainly, the paper calendar is not entirely outdated! Whatever system you adopt, be sure that it suits you, and that it is secure.

And speaking of security . . .

You will also need to have a filing system for the reams of financial and legal documents you will be required to copy and provide. These documents should not be kept any place your husband can access.

4. They have grace under pressure and attempts to provoke them fall flat.

Emotions are bound to run high during your divorce, and when they do, your best bet is always to remain calm, cool and collected. This is especially true for appearances before a judge.

Outbursts of anger can severely compromise your case—and make no mistake, your husband has told his attorney exactly what buttons to push. It is a terribly insensitive strategy, but getting you to lose your composure is a common tactic of divorce attorneys. By pressing those same buttons again, and again, and again, his side is hoping you'll lose it in front of the judge. From there, it's a short step to claiming, for example, that you have anger issues, and your temper makes you an unfit mother.

The situation can get even worse. If you've been a victim of intimate partner abuse, your husband's attorney can use your outburst to claim that in fact, your husband was the victim of *your* abuse, and anything you suffered was only him defending himself. This happens more often than you'd believe. Grace under pressure is critical, especially during custody battles and in domestic abuse cases. Figure out how you're going to achieve it, whether it's through a mantra, or breathing deeply, or some other coping mechanism.

5. **They keep their perspective and focus on the future.**

Anyone going through divorce has to keep their sights on the life that lies ahead of them. Remember that no matter how wretched things seem, this, too, shall pass, and ultimately, you and your children will be all right. There is life after divorce[6], and with the proper planning, your single life can be productive, fulfilling and financially secure and stable, as well.

Setting aside your emotions, asking for help, staying organized, keeping your cool, and maintaining perspective . . . some of this may not come naturally to you, but that doesn't mean you can't do it. Point yourself in the right direction, and keep learning and improving as you proceed ahead.If needed, you can even "fake it till you make it," as the saying goes. All of these skills are vital to the successful outcome of your divorce, and they'll serve you well in your new life as a single woman, too.

Reminder: Everybody's different, and every divorce is different, but there is much to be learned from common threads of the success stories. Get in touch with women who've been through it, and learn how they coped.

Hot tip: Remember that spyware can be installed on electronic devices. If you keep records on your laptop, or use your smartphone for email or appointment tracking, be vigilant. Make absolutely sure your husband has no access to these devices and that they don't share a network with any devices of his.

Legal matters: Cultivate the assertiveness to speak up if you have a question about why your legal team is doing something a particular way or if you have the sinking feeling that something is not going well. They are the legal experts, but they work for you, and you're entitled to know the whys and hows of the process.

CHAPTER 36

WANT MORE?

Now that you've finished reading *Divorce: Think Financially, Not Emotionally*® *Volume II*[1] and know more about what it takes to come through divorce successfully, you may be wondering, "What's next?" Once you have your divorce settlement, how can you invest it so that it lasts as long as possible? Are there specific steps you should take . . . or not take?

You're not the only one who has those kinds of questions—and that's precisely why I'm writing *Think Financially, Not Emotionally*® *- A Woman's Guide To Financial Security After Divorce*[2], to be published in late 2015. In this new addition to the *Think Financially, Not Emotionally*®[3] series, you'll find solid, easy-to-understand information about today's most pressing post-divorce topics, including:

- » The basics every woman needs to know about investing in stocks, bonds, mutual funds, ETFs, annuities, etc.
- » How to create a spending plan
- » How to establish good credit

- » The pros and cons of a reverse mortgage
- » Optimizing your social security benefit
- » The financial aspects of planning for long-term care
- » Five critical keys to estate planning
- » Using insurance to protect your assets
- » What you need to know about trusts
- » *...And much more!*

Divorce: Think Financially, Not Emotionally® - *A Woman's Guide To Financial Security After Divorce*[4] will be available in paperback and as an eBook (Kindle, Nook, PDF, etc.) in late 2015.

Visit http://ThinkFinancially.com to see all of my divorce-related books, including any new releases, and for information about online eLearning courses, live events and other resources to help you *Think Financially, Not Emotionally*[®5] before, during, and after your divorce.

APPENDIX A

DIVORCE FINANCIAL CHECKLIST

The following is a checklist of the financial information that you will need:

1. Income Tax Returns. Completed personal, corporate, partnership, joint venture, or other income tax returns (federal, state and local), including W-2, 1099, and K-1 forms, in your possession or control for the last 5 years, including all amended tax returns. Do you expect any tax refunds? ☐

   1A Business Financial Statements. Net worth statement—balance sheet or list of assets and liabilities Income statement—cash flow or income and expense statement. ☐

2. Income Information. Current income information, including payroll stubs and all other evidence of income (investment property, rental/lease agreements, dividends, interest, royalties, lottery winnings, etc.) since the filing of your last tax return. ☐

3. Personal Property Tax Returns filed in this state or anywhere else from the start of the marriage. ☐

4. Banking Information. All monthly bank statements, passbooks, check registers, deposit slips, cancelled checks, and bank charge notices on personal and business accounts, certificates of deposit, and money market and retirement accounts from banks, savings and loan institutions, credit unions, or other institutions in which you or your spouse has an interest. ☐

5. Financial Statements submitted to banks, lending institutions, or any other persons or entities, which were prepared by you or your spouse at any time during the last five (5) years. ☐

6. Loan Applications made within the last five (5) years. ☐

7. Brokerage Statements. Statements from all accounts of securities and/or commodities dealers or mutual funds maintained by you or your spouse during the marriage and held individually, jointly, or as a trustee or guardian. ☐

8. Stocks, Bonds, and Mutual Funds. Certificates, if available, of accounts owned by either spouse during the marriage or pre-owned by you. ☐

9. Stock Options. All records pertaining to stock options held in any corporation or other entity, exercised or not exercised (include any restricted stock). ☐

10. Pension, Money Purchase Plans, Profit Sharing, Employee Stock Option Plans, Deferred Compensation Agreement, and Retirement Plans (401(k), 403(b), 412(e)(3), 457, military, IRA, Roth IRA, SEP-IRA, Keogh) or any other kind of plan owned by you or by any corporation in which you and/or your spouse have been a participant during the marriage, including annual statements.

11. Wills and Trust Agreements (include any Powers of Attorney, etc.) executed by you or in which you have a present or contingent interest or in which you are a beneficiary, trustee, executor, or guardian and from which benefits have been received, are being received, or will be received and which are or were in existence during the past five (5) years, including inter vivos trusts. All records of declaration of trust and minute books for all trusts to which you are a party, including the certificates, if any, showing such interest and copies of all statements, receipts, disbursements, investments, and other transactions.

12. Life Insurance or certificate of life insurance policies now in existence, insuring your life or the life of your spouse, and statements of the cash value, if available.

13. General Insurance. Copies of insurance policies, including but not limited to annuities, health, accident, disability, casualty, motor vehicles of any kind, property liability, including contents, and insurance owned by the parties during the past five (5) years of the marriage.

14. Outstanding Debts. Documents reflecting all debts owed to you or by you (including those cosigned by you), secured or unsecured, including mortgages, personal loans, credit card statements, promissory notes and lawsuits pending or previously filed in any court. ☐

15. Business Records or ledgers in your possession and control that are either personal or business-related, together with all accounts and journals. ☐

16. Real Property. Any deeds of property in which you and/or your spouse have an interest, together with evidence of all contributions, in cash or otherwise, made by you or on your behalf, toward the acquisition of such real estate during the marriage. Include all purchase agreements, mortgages, notes, property tax statements, rental/lease agreements, appraisals and all expenses associated with each property.

    16A List of real property owned prior to your marriage as well as real property acquired during the marriage by gift and/or inheritance. ☐

17. Sale and Option Agreements on any real estate owned by you either individually, through another person or entity, jointly, or as trustee or guardian. ☐

18. Personal Property. Documents, invoices, contracts, insurance policies, and appraisals on all personal property, including furniture, fixtures, jewelry, artwork, furnishings, furs, equipment, antiques, and any type of collections (coin, stamps, gold, etc.), owned by you individually, jointly, as trustee or guardian, or through any other person or entity during the term of the marriage. ☐

18A. List of personal property owned prior to your marriage as well as personal property acquired during the marriage by gift and/or inheritance.

19. Motor Vehicles. All financing agreements and titles to all motor vehicles owned by you, individually or jointly, at any time during the last five (5) years, including airplanes, boats, automobiles, or any other types of motor vehicles.

20. Corporate Interests. All records showing any kind of personal interest in any corporation (foreign or domestic) or any other entities not evidenced by certificate or other instrument.

21. Partnership and Joint Venture Agreements to which you have been a party during the marriage.

22. Employment Records during the term of the marriage, showing evidence of wages, salaries, bonuses, commissions, raises, promotions, expense accounts, and other benefits or deductions of any kind whether in cash, stock and/or other property. All records showing any fringe benefits available to you or your spouse from any business entity including without limitation auto, travel, private aircraft, boat, apartment/home, entertainment, country club, health club/spa, educational, vacation pay, severance pay, personal living expenses, etc.

23. Employment contracts under which you or your spouse have performed services during the past five (5) years, including a list of description of any oral contracts.

24. Charge Account statements for the past five (5) years. ☐

25. Membership cards or documents identifying participation rights in any country clubs, health clubs/spas, key clubs, private clubs, associations, or fraternal group organizations during the past five (5) years of the marriage, together with all monthly statements. ☐

26. Judgments and pleadings in which you have been a party to, either as Plaintiff or Defendant, during the marriage, including any Personal Injury Awards. ☐

27. Appraisals of any asset owned by you for the past five (5) years. ☐

28. Safe Deposit Boxes. Include a list of its contents. ☐

29. Mileage/travel awards. Provide statements of all awards both granted and used and any dates of expiration. ☐

30. Anything else that you think may be an asset. ☐

ACKNOWLEDGMENTS

I would like to offer my thanks and gratitude to the following people:

Amy Osmond Cook, Publisher of Sourced Media Books, who took my manuscript and did a fantastic job of turning it into the book you now hold.

Bill Greaves, who did an amazing job with the book cover design.

Kathy Siranosian and Susan Sundermeyer, who helped me turn my ideas, expertise, and grammatically incorrect writing into a terrific manuscript. I could not have done it without them.

Laura Wasser, Sonja Morgan, and Liz Smith, who were kind enough to read my manuscript and provide me with some great blurbs for this book. I very much appreciate their generosity.

My clients, who inspired me to write this book.

And special thanks to my wife and daughters for their ongoing love and support.

ABOUT THE AUTHOR

Jeffrey A. Landers, CDFA™, is the founder of Bedrock Divorce Advisors, LLC, a divorce financial advisory firm that works exclusively with women throughout the United States, and ThinkFinancially. com, a website created to educate, empower, and support women before, during, and after divorce.

He writes a weekly blog for Forbes.com on the financial aspects of divorce for women called "Divorce Dollars and Sense" and contributes articles regularly to *The Huffington Post*, DailyWorth, More. com, Lawyers.com, and many others.

Jeff has also been extensively interviewed about the financial aspects of divorce for women by CBS Television News and such prestigious publications as *The Wall Street Journal, Dow Jones, The Miami Herald, Smart Money, Consumer Reports, The Christian Science Monitor,* and many others.

Jeff earned his BA degree in psychology from Columbia University and studied law at Pace University School of Law before becoming a divorce financial advisor.

He enjoys running, practicing Kung-Fu, and spending time with his family.

ENDNOTES

Introduction

1. Think Financially, Not Emotionally®. http://thinkfinancially.com/.

Chapter 1

1. "About Bedrock Divorce Advisors." Bedrock Divorce Advisors™, LLC. http://www.bedrockdivorce.com/about.php.

2. Landers, Jeff. "Divorcing Women: Here's Where Husbands Typically Hide Assets." Forbes. March 14, 2012. http://www.forbes.com/sites/jefflanders/2012/03/14/divorcing-women-heres-where-husbands-typically-hide-assets/.

3. Landers, Jeff. "What Divorcing Women Need To Know About Alimony 'Reform.'" Forbes. May 17, 2013. http://www.forbes.com/sites/jefflanders/2013/05/17/what-divorcing-women-need-to-know-about-alimony-reform/.

4. "Marilyn B. Chinitz, Partner." Blank Rome LLP. http://blankrome.com/index.cfm?contentID=10&bioID=5077.

5. "I'm Getting Divorced – Can I Still Collect Social Security Retirement Benefits Based On My Husband's Earnings?" Bedrock Divorce Advisors™, LLC. March 1, 2011. http://bedrockdivorce.com/blog/?p=134.

6. Perez, William. "Single Filing Status." About.com. http://taxes.about.com/od/filingstatus/qt/single.htm.

7. Think Financially, Not Emotionally®. http://thinkfinancially.com/.

Chapter 2

1. Landers, Jeff. "What A Divorcing Woman Needs To Know About Her Husband's Cash-Based Business." Forbes. January 30, 2013. http://www.forbes.com/sites/jefflanders/2013/01/30/what-a-divorcing-woman-needs-to-know-about-her-husbands-cash-based-business/.

2. "How To Find a Divorce Attorney, Divorce Financial Planner and Other Members of Your Divorce Team." Bedrock Divorce Advisors™, LLC. June 1, 2011. http://www.bedrockdivorce.com/blog/?p=275.

3. Landers, Jeff. "Financial Strategies for Divorcing A Narcissist." Forbes. December 11, 2012. http://www.forbes.com/sites/jefflanders/2012/12/11/financial-strategies-for-divorcing-a-narcissist/.

4. Landers, Jeff. "My Best Financial Advice for the Bride-to-Be." Forbes. June 28, 2012. http://www.forbes.com/sites/jefflanders/2012/06/28/my-best-financial-advice-for-the-bride-to-be/.

5. Ibid.

6. Landers, Jeff. "What Are the Consequences Of Hiding Assets During Divorce?" Forbes. November 14, 2012. http://www.forbes.com/sites/jefflanders/2012/11/14/what-are-the-consequences-of-hiding-assets-during-divorce/.

7. Landers, Jeff. "Small World, Big Problem: Divorces Involving Dual Citizenship." Forbes. January 10, 2013. http://www.forbes.com/sites/jefflanders/2013/01/10/small-world-big-problem-divorces-involving-dual-citizenship/.

8. Think Financially, Not Emotionally®. http://thinkfinancially.com/.

9. Landers, Jeff. "The Five Key Points Divorcing Women Need to Know About Financial Affidavits." Forbes. May 9, 2012. http://www.forbes.com/sites/jefflanders/2012/05/09/the-five-key-points-divorcing-women-need-to-know-about-financial-affidavits/.

10. "The Difference Between Separate and Marital Property." Bedrock Divorce Advisors™, LLC. June 8, 2011. http://www.bedrockdivorce.com/blog/?p=293.

ENDNOTES

Chapter 3

1. Landers, Jeff. "Legal Separation or Divorce: Which is Better Financially?" Forbes. January 10, 2012. http://www.forbes.com/sites/jefflanders/2012/01/10/legal-separation-or-divorce-which-is-better-financially/.

2. Landers, Jeff. "Divorcing Women: Here's What You Need to Know About ATROs." Forbes. July 11, 2012. http://www.forbes.com/sites/jefflanders/2012/07/11/divorcing-women-heres-what-you-need-to-know-about-atros/.

Chapter 4

1. "The Secret To Surviving Divorce With Your Finances Intact." Bedrock Divorce Advisors™, LLC. May 17, 2011. http://www.bedrockdivorce.com/blog/?page_id=266.

2. "Marilyn B. Chinitz, Partner." Blank Rome LLP. http://blankrome.com/index.cfm?contentID=10&bioID=5077.

3. "Profiles: Debra DiMaggio." The Law Offices of Debra DiMaggio. http://www.dimaggio-law.com/profiles.html.

4. "Attorney & Paralegal Profiles: Laura A. Wasser." Law Offices of Wasser, Cooperman & Carter. http://www.wccfamilylaw.com/attorney-staff-profiles/laura-wasser/.

5. "It Doesn't Have to Be That Way: How to Divorce Without Destroying Your Family or Bankrupting Yourself." Amazon. http://www.amazon.com/Doesnt-Have-That-Way-Bankrupting/dp/1250029783/ref=sr_1_1?ie=UTF8&qid=1370358147&sr=8-1&keywords=laura+wasser.

6. "About Kelly Chang Rickert." Law Offices of Kelly Chang. http://www.purposedrivenlawyers.com/KellyChang.html.

7. "Jennifer A. Brandt." Cozen O'Connor. http://www.cozen.com/people/bios/brandt-jennifer.

8. "Bari Zell Weinberger Profile." Weinberger Law Group, LLC. http://www.weinbergerlawgroup.com/newjersey-attorneys/bari-zell-weinberger.aspx.

9. Landers, Jeff. "Financial Strategies for Divorcing A Narcissist." Forbes. December 11, 2012. http://www.forbes.com/sites/jefflanders/2012/12/11/financial-strategies-for-divorcing-a-narcissist/.

10. Think Financially, Not Emotionally®. http://thinkfinancially.com/.

Chapter 5

1. Landers, Jeff. "Five Financial Lessons Women Can Learn from the Demi and Ashton Break-up Rumors." Forbes. October 25, 2011. http://www.forbes.com/sites/jefflanders/2011/10/25/five-financial-lessons-women-can-learn-from-the-demi-and-ashton-break-up-rumors/.

2. Landers, Jeff. "Does Maria Shriver Have A Prenup? Why Did Arnold Put His Movie Career On Hold?" Forbes. May 25, 2011. http://www.forbes.com/sites/jefflanders/2011/05/25/does-maria-shriver-have-a-prenup-why-did-arnold-put-his-movie-career-on-hold/.

3. "Frankel and Hoppy uncomfortable living situation escalates divorce drama." Examiner. May 2, 2013. http://www.examiner.com/article/frankel-and-hoppy-uncomfortable-living-situation-escalates-divorce-drama.

4. "The Difference Between Separate and Marital Property." Bedrock Divorce Advisors™, LLC. June 8, 2011. http://www.bedrockdivorce.com/blog/?p=293.

5. "Attorneys: Judith L. Poller." Pryor Cashman LLP. http://www.pryorcashman.com/attorneys-187.html.

6. "Bari Zell Weinberger Profile." Weinberger Law Group, LLC. http://www.weinbergerlawgroup.com/newjersey-attorneys/bari-zell-weinberger.aspx.

7. "Attorney & Paralegal Profiles: Laura A. Wasser." Law Offices of Wasser, Cooperman & Carter. http://www.wccfamilylaw.com/attorney-staff-profiles/laura-wasser/.

8. "It Doesn't Have to Be That Way: How to Divorce Without Destroying Your Family or Bankrupting Yourself." Amazon. http://www.amazon.com/Doesnt-Have-That-Way-Bankrupting/dp/1250029783/ref=sr_1_1?ie=UTF8&qid=1370358147&sr=8-1&keywords=laura+wasser.

9. "Do You Live in a Community Property State or an Equitable Distribution State?" Bedrock Divorce Advisors™, LLC. June 16, 2011. http://www.bedrockdivorce.com/blog/?p=296.

Chapter 6

1. "Financial Information Checklist." Bedrock Divorce Advisors™, LLC. http://bedrockdivorce.com/Financial-information-checklist.pdf.

2. Landers, Jeff. "Good News For Divorcing Women: Credit Reform, Reformed!" Forbes. May 7, 2013. http://www.forbes.com/sites/jefflanders/2013/05/07/good-news-for-divorcing-women-credit-reform-reformed/.

3. Landers, Jeff. "Pros And Cons Of Keeping A Secret Fund In Case You Divorce." Forbes. February 14, 2013. http://www.forbes.com/sites/jefflanders/2013/02/14/pros-and-cons-of-keeping-a-secret-fund-in-case-you-divorce/.

4. Bedrock Divorce Advisors™, LLC. http://www.bedrockdivorce.com/.

5. Think Financially, Not Emotionally®. http://thinkfinancially.com/.

6. Landers, Jeff. "Expert Advice For Divorcing Women: Coping Emotionally, While You're Thinking Financially." Forbes. May 1, 2013. http://www.forbes.com/sites/jefflanders/2013/05/01/expert-advice-for-divorcing-women-coping-emotionally-while-youre-thinking-financially/.

Chapter 7

1. "Attorney & Paralegal Profiles: Laura A. Wasser." Law Offices of Wasser, Cooperman & Carter. http://www.wccfamilylaw.com/attorney-staff-profiles/laura-wasser/.

2. Landers, Jeff. "How 'Conflicting Out' Top Divorce Attorneys Can Impact Your Divorce." Forbes. April 17, 2012. http://www.forbes.com/sites/jefflanders/2012/04/17/how-conflicting-out-top-divorce-attorneys-can-impact-your-divorce/.

3. "It Doesn't Have to Be That Way: How to Divorce Without Destroying Your Family or Bankrupting Yourself." Amazon. http://www.amazon.com/Doesnt-Have-That-Way-Bankrupting/dp/1250029783/ref=sr_1_1?ie=UTF8&qid=1370358147&sr=8-1&keywords=laura+wasser.

4. "Profiles: Debra DiMaggio." The Law Offices of Debra DiMaggio. http://www.dimaggio-law.com/profiles.html.

5. "How To Find a Divorce Attorney, Divorce Financial Planner and Other Members of Your Divorce Team." Bedrock Divorce Advisors™, LLC. June 1, 2011. http://www.bedrockdivorce.com/blog/?p=275.

6. "About Bedrock Divorce Advisors." Bedrock Divorce Advisors™, LLC. http://www.bedrockdivorce.com/about.php.

7. Landers, Jeff. "Four Reasons Why A Woman Needs A Vocational Expert On Her Divorce Team." Forbes. October 24, 2012. http://www.forbes.com/sites/jefflanders/2012/10/24/four-reasons-why-a-woman-needs-a-vocational-expert-on-her-divorce-team/.

8. "Financial Information Checklist." Bedrock Divorce Advisors™, LLC. http://bedrockdivorce.com/Financial-information-checklist.pdf.

9. Landers, Jeff. "Divorcing Women: Here's Where Husbands Typically Hide Assets." Forbes. March 14, 2012. http://www.forbes.com/sites/jefflanders/2012/03/14/divorcing-women-heres-where-husbands-typically-hide-assets/.

10. Landers, Jeff. "Divorcing Women: Here's What You Need to Know About ATROs." Forbes. July 11, 2012. http://www.forbes.com/sites/jefflanders/2012/07/11/divorcing-women-heres-what-you-need-to-know-about-atros/.

11. Think Financially, Not Emotionally®. http://thinkfinancially.com/.

12. "How To Find a Divorce Attorney, Divorce Financial Planner and Other Members of Your Divorce Team." Bedrock Divorce Advisors™, LLC. June 1, 2011. http://www.bedrockdivorce.com/blog/?p=275.

13. Landers, Jeff. "Pros And Cons Of Keeping A Secret Fund In Case You Divorce." Forbes. February 14, 2013. http://www.forbes.com/

sites/jefflanders/2013/02/14/pros-and-cons-of-keeping-a-secret-fund-in-case-you-divorce/.

Chapter 8

1. "Bedrock Divorce Advisors™, LLC." Facebook. https://www.facebook.com/BedrockDivorce.

2. @bedrock_divorce (Jeff Landers). Twitter. https://twitter.com/bedrock_divorce.

3. Instagram. http://www.instagram.com.

4. "Jeff Landers." LinkedIn. http://www.linkedin.com/in/jefflanders/.

5. "Facebook and Twitter Play Big Roles in Divorces [Infographic]." Lawyers.com. July 31, 2013. http://blogs.lawyers.com/2013/07/divorce-and-social-media-infographic/?cid=emm:100.

6. Hutul, Pamela J. and Michelle Lowrance. "Social Media in Divorce Proceedings." Family Lawyer Magazine. July 19, 2013. http://www.familylawyermagazine.com/articles/social-media-in-divorce-proceedings.

7. Foursquare. https://foursquare.com.

8. Landers, Jeff. "The Five Key Points Divorcing Women Need to Know About Financial Affidavits." Forbes. May 9, 2012. http://www.forbes.com/sites/jefflanders/2012/05/09/the-five-key-points-divorcing-women-need-to-know-about-financial-affidavits/.

Chapter 9

1. Think Financially, Not Emotionally®. http://thinkfinancially.com/.

2. "About Tiips: Dr. Kaminski Bio." The Institute of Integrative Psychiatry. http://www.tiips.org/dr-kaminski-bio/.

3. Kristin Davin, Psy.D. http://www.kristindavin.com.

4. "Find a Therapist." Psychology Today. http://therapists.psychologytoday.com/rms/?gclid=CPTSuKnEmbkCFQee4Aodp3gAgw.

5. "Find a Therapist." NetworkTherapy.com http://www.network-therapy.com/directory/find_therapist.asp?gclid=COau3NHEmbkCFQSk4AodQVsA2w.

6. GoodTherapy.org. http://www.goodtherapy.org/.

7. "The Secret To Surviving Divorce With Your Finances Intact." Bedrock Divorce Advisors™, LLC. May 17, 2011. http://www.bedrockdivorce.com/blog/?page_id=266.

Chapter 10

1. Bedrock Divorce Advisors™, LLC. "Do You Live in a Community Property State or an Equitable Distribution State?" June 16, 2011. http://www.bedrockdivorce.com/blog/?p=296.

2. "How Are Appreciated Assets Divided in a Divorce?" Bedrock Divorce Advisors™, LLC. June 28, 2011. http://www.bedrockdivorce.com/blog/?p=312.

3. Abkowitz, Alyssa. "Appraisers in Splitsville." The Wall Street Journal. November 29, 2012. http://online.wsj.com/article/SB10001424127887324851704578133200609815808.html?mod=real_estate_newsreel.

4. "How To Find a Divorce Attorney, Divorce Financial Planner and Other Members of Your Divorce Team." Bedrock Divorce Advisors™, LLC. June 1, 2011. http://www.bedrockdivorce.com/blog/?p=275.

Chapter 12

1. Think Financially, Not Emotionally®. http://thinkfinancially.com/.

2. Landers, Jeff. "Pros And Cons Of Keeping A Secret Fund In Case You Divorce." Forbes. February 14, 2013. http://www.forbes.com/sites/jefflanders/2013/02/14/pros-and-cons-of-keeping-a-secret-fund-in-case-you-divorce/.

3. "Financial Information Checklist." Bedrock Divorce Advisors™, LLC. http://bedrockdivorce.com/Financial-information-checklist.pdf.

4. "How To Find a Divorce Attorney, Divorce Financial Planner and Other Members of Your Divorce Team." Bedrock Divorce Advisors™, LLC. June 1, 2011. http://www.bedrockdivorce.com/blog/?p=275.

5. Think Financially, Not Emotionally®. http://thinkfinancially.com/.

Chapter 13

1. "Divorce financial strategy services." Bedrock Divorce Advisors™, LLC. http://www.bedrockdivorce.com/services.php.

Chapter 15

1. Landers, Jeff. "My Best Financial Advice for the Bride-to-Be." Forbes. June 28, 2012. http://www.forbes.com/sites/jefflanders/2012/06/28/my-best-financial-advice-for-the-bride-to-be/.

2. "The Difference Between Separate and Marital Property." Bedrock Divorce Advisors™, LLC. June 8, 2011. http://www.bedrockdivorce.com/blog/?p=293.

3. Think Financially, Not Emotionally®. http://thinkfinancially.com/.

4. Landers, Jeff. "Divorcing Women: Here's Where Husbands Typically Hide Assets." Forbes. March 14, 2012. http://www.forbes.com/sites/jefflanders/2012/03/14/divorcing-women-heres-where-husbands-typically-hide-assets/.

5. Landers, Jeff. "21 Signs That Your Husband May Be Hiding Marital Assets During Your Divorce." Forbes. March 20, 2012. http://www.forbes.com/sites/jefflanders/2012/03/20/21-signs-that-your-husband-may-be-hiding-marital-assets-during-your-divorce/.

Chapter 16

1. "The Difference Between Separate and Marital Property." Bedrock Divorce Advisors™, LLC. June 8, 2011. http://www.bedrockdivorce.com/blog/?p=293.

2. "Do You Live in a Community Property State or an Equitable Distribution State?" Bedrock Divorce Advisors™, LLC. June 16, 2011. http://www.bedrockdivorce.com/blog/?p=296.

3. Think Financially, Not Emotionally®. http://thinkfinancially.com/.

Chapter 17

1. Landers, Jeff. "Why Divorcing Women Need to Pay Careful Attention to the Date of Separation." Forbes. September 28, 2011. http://www.forbes.com/sites/jefflanders/2011/09/28/why-divorcing-women-need-to-pay-careful-attention-to-the-date-of-separation/.

2. "Miles Mason, Sr. | Memphis Divorce Lawyer & Family Law Attorney." Miles Mason Family Law Group, PLC. http://memphisdivorce.com/about-us/meet-the-team/miles-mason-sr/.

3. Bedrock Divorce Advisors™, LLC. http://www.bedrockdivorce.com/.

Chapter 18

1. "The Difference Between Separate and Marital Property." Bedrock Divorce Advisors™, LLC. June 8, 2011. http://www.bedrockdivorce.com/blog/?p=293.

2. "Do You Live in a Community Property State or an Equitable Distribution State?" Bedrock Divorce Advisors™, LLC. June 16, 2011. http://www.bedrockdivorce.com/blog/?p=296.

3. "How To Find a Divorce Attorney, Divorce Financial Planner and Other Members of Your Divorce Team." Bedrock Divorce Advisors™, LLC. June 1, 2011. http://www.bedrockdivorce.com/blog/?p=275.

4. Landers, Jeff. "Divorcing Women: Will The New Tax Laws Impact Your Divorce Settlement?" Forbes. February 20, 2013. http://www.forbes.com/sites/jefflanders/2013/02/20/divorcing-women-will-the-new-tax-laws-impact-your-divorce-settlement/.

5. Think Financially, Not Emotionally®. http://thinkfinancially.com/.

Chapter 19

1. "Pets by the Numbers." The Humane Society of the United States. January 30, 2014. http://www.humanesociety.org/issues/pet_overpopulation/facts/pet_ownership_statistics.html.

2. Jasmin. "Divorce in America [infographic]." Daily Infographic. October 24, 2013. http://dailyinfographic.com/divorce-in-america-infographic.

3. Think Financially, Not Emotionally®. http://thinkfinancially.com/.

4. Davis, Jeanie Lerche. "5 Ways Pets Can Improve Your Health." WebMD. http://www.webmd.com/hypertension-high-blood-pressure/features/health-benefits-of-pets.

5. Landers, Jeff. "Skittish About A Prenup? Like It Or Not, You Already Have One." Forbes. July 17, 2013. http://www.forbes.com/sites/jefflanders/2013/07/17/skittish-about-a-prenup-like-it-or-not-you-already-have-one/.

Chapter 20

1. Think Financially, Not Emotionally®. http://thinkfinancially.com/.

2. "Rewards Terms & Conditions." Marriott. http://www.marriott.com/rewards/terms/default.mi.

3. Think Financially, Not Emotionally®. http://thinkfinancially.com/.

Chapter 21

1. "The Difference Between Separate and Marital Property." Bedrock Divorce Advisors™, LLC. June 8, 2011. http://www.bedrockdivorce.com/blog/?p=293.

2. "Do You Live in a Community Property State or an Equitable Distribution State?" Bedrock Divorce Advisors™, LLC. June 16, 2011. http://www.bedrockdivorce.com/blog/?p=296.

3. Landers, Jeff. "Four Reasons Why A Woman Needs A Vocational Expert On Her Divorce Team." Forbes. October 24, 2012. http://www.forbes.com/sites/jefflanders/2012/10/24/four-reasons-why-a-woman-needs-a-vocational-expert-on-her-divorce-team/.

4. Landers, Jeff. "Skittish About A Prenup? Like It Or Not, You Already Have One." Forbes. July 17, 2013. http://www.forbes.com/sites/jefflanders/2013/07/17/skittish-about-a-prenup-like-it-or-not-you-already-have-one/.

Chapter 22

1. Bedrock Divorce Advisors™, LLC. http://www.bedrockdivorce. com/.

Chapter 23

1. "How To Find a Divorce Attorney, Divorce Financial Planner and Other Members of Your Divorce Team." Bedrock Divorce Advisors™, LLC. June 1, 2011. http://www.bedrockdivorce.com/blog/?p=275.

2. Landers, Jeff. "21 Signs That Your Husband May Be Hiding Marital Assets During Your Divorce." Forbes. March 20, 2012. http://www. forbes.com/sites/jefflanders/2012/03/20/21-signs-that-your-hus-band-may-be-hiding-marital-assets-during-your-divorce/.

3. Miles Mason Family Law Group, PLC. http://memphisdivorce. com/.

4. Mason, Sr., Miles. "The Forensic Accounting Deskbook: A Practical Guide to Financial Investigation and Analysis for Family Lawyers." http://forensicaccountingdeskbook.com/.

5. Landers, Jeff. "Why a Lifestyle Analysis Is So Critically Important For Divorcing Women." Forbes. February 14, 2012. http://www. forbes.com/sites/jefflanders/2012/02/14/why-a-lifestyle-analysis-is-so-critically-important-for-divorcing-women/.

6. Bedrock Divorce Advisors™, LLC. http://www.bedrockdivorce. com/.

7. "Divorce financial strategy services." Bedrock Divorce Advisors™, LLC. http://www.bedrockdivorce.com/services.php.

Chapter 24

1. Landers, Jeff. "Divorcing Women: Here's Where Husbands Typically Hide Assets." Forbes. March 14, 2012. http://www.forbes.com/ sites/jefflanders/2012/03/14/divorcing-women-heres-where-hus-bands-typically-hide-assets/.

2. "Miles Mason, Sr. | Memphis Divorce Lawyer & Family Law Attorney." Miles Mason Family Law Group, PLC. http://memphisdivorce. com/about-us/meet-the-team/miles-mason-sr/.

3. "The Tennessee Divorce Client's Handbook: What Every Divorcing Spouse Needs to Know." Miles Mason Family Law Group, PLC. http://www.memphisdivorce.com/the-tennessee-divorce-clients-handbook/.

Chapter 25

1. "Three in 10 Americans Admit to Financial Deception with Partners." National Endowment for Financial Education. January 14, 2011. http://www.nefe.org/press-room/news/admitting-to-financial-deceptions.aspx.

2. "Federal Rules of Civil Procedure." Wikipedia. http://en.wikipedia. org/wiki/Federal_Rules_of_Civil_Procedure.

3. Landers, Jeff. "The Five Key Points Divorcing Women Need to Know About Financial Affidavits." Forbes. May 9, 2012. http://www. forbes.com/sites/jefflanders/2012/05/09/the-five-key-points-divorcing-women-need-to-know-about-financial-affidavits/.

4. O'Neill, Ann W. "Ex-Wife Loses Big in This Game of Chance." LA Times. November 17, 1999. http://articles.latimes.com/1999/nov/17/ news/mn-34537.

5. "The Difference Between Separate and Marital Property." Bedrock Divorce Advisors™, LLC. June 8, 2011. http://www.bedrockdivorce. com/blog/?p=293.

6. Think Financially, Not Emotionally®. http://thinkfinancially.com/.

7. Landers, Jeff. "Why a Lifestyle Analysis Is So Critically Important For Divorcing Women." Forbes. February 14, 2012. http://www. forbes.com/sites/jefflanders/2012/02/14/why-a-lifestyle-analysis-is-so-critically-important-for-divorcing-women/.

8. Bedrock Divorce Advisors™, LLC. http://www.bedrockdivorce. com/.

9. Stim, Rich. "Problems of Hidden Assets in Michigan Divorce Litigation." DivorceNet. http://www.divorcenet.com/states/michigan/problems_of_hidden_assets.

Chapter 26

1. "How To Find a Divorce Attorney, Divorce Financial Planner and Other Members of Your Divorce Team." Bedrock Divorce Advisors™, LLC. June 1, 2011. http://www.bedrockdivorce.com/blog/?p=275.

2. "The Difference Between Separate and Marital Property." Bedrock Divorce Advisors™, LLC. June 8, 2011. http://www.bedrockdivorce.com/blog/?p=293.

3. Landers, Jeff. "My Best Financial Advice for the Bride-to-Be." Forbes. June 28, 2012. http://www.forbes.com/sites/jefflanders/2012/06/28/my-best-financial-advice-for-the-bride-to-be/.

Chapter 27

1. "National Marriage and Divorce Rate Trends." Centers for Disease Control and Prevention. http://www.cdc.gov/nchs/nvss/marriage_divorce_tables.htm.

2. "How To Find a Divorce Attorney, Divorce Financial Planner and Other Members of Your Divorce Team." Bedrock Divorce Advisors™, LLC. June 1, 2011. http://www.bedrockdivorce.com/blog/?p=275.

3. Think Financially, Not Emotionally®. http://thinkfinancially.com/.

4. Landers, Jeff. "The Five Key Points Divorcing Women Need to Know About Financial Affidavits." Forbes. May 9, 2012. http://www.forbes.com/sites/jefflanders/2012/05/09/the-five-key-points-divorcing-women-need-to-know-about-financial-affidavits/.

5. Landers, Jeff. "Deciding To Become A Stay-At-Home Mom? Consider This Cautionary Tale." Forbes. May 29, 2014. http://www.forbes.com/sites/jefflanders/2014/05/29/deciding-to-become-a-sahm-stay-at-home-mom-consider-this-cautionary-tale/.

Chapter 28

1. Bedrock Divorce Advisors™, LLC. http://www.bedrockdivorce. com/.

2. Landers, Jeff. "Upfront Lump Sum Payment or Alimony? Why Some NFL Ex-Wives Are Now Smiling." Forbes. June 1, 2011. http:// www.forbes.com/sites/jefflanders/2011/06/01/upfront-lump-sum-payment-or-alimony-why-some-nfl-ex-wives-are-now-smiling/.

3. "Marilyn B. Chinitz, Partner." Blank Rome LLP. http://blankrome. com/index.cfm?contentID=10&bioID=5077.

4. "Compilation Of The Social Security Laws: Title IV." Social Security Administration. http://www.ssa.gov/OP_Home/ssact/title04/0400.htm.

5. Landers, Jeff. "How Divorcing Women Should Handle Retirement Accounts And Pension Plans." Forbes. June 13, 2012. http://www. forbes.com/sites/jefflanders/2012/06/13/how-divorcing-women-should-handle-retirement-accounts-and-pension-plans/.

6. Boulette, Michael P. "Collecting Child Support & Maintenance: A New Role for QDROs." Bench & Bar of Minnesota. October 16, 2012. http://mnbenchbar.com/2012/10/collecting-child-support/.

7. "Using a QDRO to Collect Support Payments." American Bar Association. http://www.americanbar.org/content/dam/aba/publishing/family_law_enewsletter/OrtizArticle.authcheckdam.pdf.

8. "How To Find a Divorce Attorney, Divorce Financial Planner and Other Members of Your Divorce Team." Bedrock Divorce Advisors™, LLC. June 1, 2011. http://www.bedrockdivorce.com/blog/?p=275.

Chapter 29

1. "Frequently Asked Questions: Qualified Domestic Relations Orders." United States Department of Labor. http://www.dol.gov/ebsa/faqs/faq_qdro.html.

2. Landers, Jeff. "How Divorcing Women Should Handle Retirement Accounts And Pension Plans." Forbes. June 13, 2012. http://www. forbes.com/sites/jefflanders/2012/06/13/how-divorcing-women-should-handle-retirement-accounts-and-pension-plans/.

3. "Retirement Plans, Benefits & Savings." United States Department of Labor. http://www.dol.gov/dol/topic/retirement/erisa.htm.

4. "Attorney Bio: Matthew L. Lundy." Matthew Lundy Law. http://www.mlundylaw.com/Attorney_Profile.html.

5. "How To Find a Divorce Attorney, Divorce Financial Planner and Other Members of Your Divorce Team." Bedrock Divorce Advisors™, LLC. June 1, 2011. http://www.bedrockdivorce.com/blog/?p=275.

6. "The Employee Retirement Income Security Act (ERISA)." United States Department of Labor. http://www.dol.gov/compliance/laws/comp-erisa.htm.

7. "Retirement Plans, Benefits & Savings." United States Department of Labor. http://www.dol.gov/dol/topic/retirement/erisa.htm.

8. "Bari Zell Weinberger Profile." Weinberger Law Group, LLC. http://www.weinbergerlawgroup.com/newjersey-attorneys/bari-zell-weinberger.aspx.

Chapter 30

1. Landers, Jeff. "Upfront Lump Sum Payment or Alimony? Why Some NFL Ex-Wives Are Now Smiling." Forbes. June 1, 2011. http://www.forbes.com/sites/jefflanders/2011/06/01/upfront-lump-sum-payment-or-alimony-why-some-nfl-ex-wives-are-now-smiling/.

2. Bedrock Divorce Advisors™, LLC. http://www.bedrockdivorce.com/.

3. Landers, Jeff. "June Brides, Are You Ready for Divorce?" Forbes. June 7, 2011. http://www.forbes.com/sites/jefflanders/2011/06/07/june-brides-are-you-ready-for-divorce/.

4. Landers, Jeff. "Deciding To Become A Stay-At-Home Mom? Consider This Cautionary Tale." Forbes. May 29, 2014. http://www.forbes.com/sites/jefflanders/2014/05/29/deciding-to-become-a-sahm-stay-at-home-mom-consider-this-cautionary-tale/.

ENDNOTES

Chapter 31

1. Bedrock Divorce Advisors™, LLC. http://www.bedrockdivorce. com/.

2. "Bari Zell Weinberger Profile." Weinberger Law Group, LLC. http://www.weinbergerlawgroup.com/newjersey-attorneys/bari-zell-weinberger.aspx.

3. Landers, Jeff. "What Divorcing Women Need To Know About Alimony 'Reform.'" Forbes. May 17, 2013. http://www.forbes.com/sites/jefflanders/2013/05/17/what-divorcing-women-need-to-know-about-alimony-reform/.

4. Landers, Jeff. "Five Reasons Your Prenup Might Be Invalid." Forbes. http://www.forbes.com/sites/jefflanders/2013/04/02/five-reasons-your-prenup-might-be-invalid/. April 2, 2013.

5. Landers, Jeff. "Court Ruling: Postnup Does Not Waive Spousal Rights To 401(K)." Forbes. August 14, 2013. http://www.forbes.com/sites/jefflanders/2013/08/14/court-ruling-postnup-does-not-waive-spousal-rights-to-401k/.

6. Landers, Jeff. "My Best Financial Advice for the Bride-to-Be." Forbes. June 28, 2012. http://www.forbes.com/sites/jefflanders/2012/06/28/my-best-financial-advice-for-the-bride-to-be/.

7. Landers, Jeff. "Four Reasons Why A Woman Needs A Vocational Expert On Her Divorce Team." Forbes. October 24, 2012. http://www.forbes.com/sites/jefflanders/2012/10/24/four-reasons-why-a-woman-needs-a-vocational-expert-on-her-divorce-team/.

Chapter 32

1. Jayson, Sharon. "More wives earning more than their spouse." USA Today. March 1, 2013. http://www.usatoday.com/story/news/nation/2013/03/01/dual-earner-couples-recession/1957621/.

2. "How To Divorce-Proof Your Business: The Prenup." Bedrock Divorce Advisors™, LLC. January 25, 2011. http://www.bedrockdivorce.com/blog/?page_id=94.

3. "Bari Zell Weinberger Profile." Weinberger Law Group, LLC. http://www.weinbergerlawgroup.com/newjersey-attorneys/bari-zell-weinberger.aspx.

4. Landers, Jeff. "Pros And Cons Of Keeping A Secret Fund In Case You Divorce." Forbes. February 14, 2013. http://www.forbes.com/sites/jefflanders/2013/02/14/pros-and-cons-of-keeping-a-secret-fund-in-case-you-divorce/.

5. Landers, Jeff. "Divorce-Proof Your Business, Even If You're Still Single Or Happily Married!" Forbes. April 19, 2011. http://www.forbes.com/sites/jefflanders/2011/04/19/divorce-proof-your-business-even-if-youre-still-single-or-happily-married/.

6. Think Financially, Not Emotionally®. http://thinkfinancially.com/.

7. The National Domestic Violence Hotline. http://www.thehotline.org/.

Chapter 33

1. Morley, Jeremy. "Expert Testimony in International Law Cases." The Law Office of Jeremy D. Morley: International Family Law. http://www.international-divorce.com/expert-testimony-in-international-family-law-cases.

2. "International Family Law Practice, 2014 ed." Thomson Reuters™. http://store.westlaw.com/international-family-law-practice-2012/179716/40816680/productdetail.

3. "The Hague Abduction Convention: Practical Issues and Procedures for Family Lawyers." American Bar Association. http://apps.americanbar.org/abastore/index.cfm?pid=5130190&section=main&fm=Product.AddToCart.

4. "How To Find a Divorce Attorney, Divorce Financial Planner and Other Members of Your Divorce Team." Bedrock Divorce Advisors™, LLC. June 1, 2011. http://www.bedrockdivorce.com/blog/?p=275.

5. Dolak, Kevin. "Kelly Rutherford Feared Abduction During Custody Battle." ABC News. September 14, 2012. http://abcnews.go.com/blogs/entertainment/2012/09/kelly-rutherford-feared-abduction-during-custody-battle/.

Chapter 34

1. Bedrock Divorce Advisors™, LLC. http://www.bedrockdivorce.com/.

2. Landers, Jeff. "Divorcing Women: Here's Where Husbands Typically Hide Assets." Forbes. March 14, 2012. http://www.forbes.com/sites/jefflanders/2012/03/14/divorcing-women-heres-where-husbands-typically-hide-assets/.

3. "Lawyers Finding Divorce App in Smart Phones: Survey of Nation's Top Attorneys Reveals Spike in Smart Phone and Text Evidence During Divorces." American Academy of Matrimonial Lawyers. February 8, 2012. http://www.aaml.org/about-the-academy/press/press-releases/divorce/lawyers-finding-divorce-app-smart-phones.

4. "Big Surge in Social Networking Evidence Says Survey of Nation's Top Divorce Lawyers: Facebook is Primary Source for Compromising Information." PR Newswire. February 10, 2010. http://www.prnewswire.com/news-releases/big-surge-in-social-networking-evidence-says-survey-of-nations-top-divorce-lawyers-84025732.html.

5. Think Financially, Not Emotionally®. http://thinkfinancially.com/.

Chapter 35

1. Landers, Jeff. "This Domestic Violence Awareness Month, Begin To Secure Your Financial Future." Forbes. October 23, 2013. http://www.forbes.com/sites/jefflanders/2013/10/23/this-domestic-violence-awareness-month-begin-to-secure-your-financial-future/.

2. Landers, Jeff. "Financial Strategies for Divorcing A Narcissist." Forbes. December 11, 2012. http://www.forbes.com/sites/jefflanders/2012/12/11/financial-strategies-for-divorcing-a-narcissist/.

3. Think Financially, Not Emotionally®. http://thinkfinancially.com/.

4. Ibid.

5. "How To Find a Divorce Attorney, Divorce Financial Planner and Other Members of Your Divorce Team." Bedrock Divorce Advisors™, LLC. June 1, 2011. http://www.bedrockdivorce.com/blog/?p=275.

6. Landers, Jeff. "Divorcing Women: Don't Forget To Update These Key Documents." Forbes. December 4, 2013. http://www.forbes.com/sites/jefflanders/2013/12/04/divorcing-women-dont-forget-to-update-these-key-documents/.

Chapter 36

1. Think Financially, Not Emotionally®. http://thinkfinancially.com/.

2. Ibid.

3. Ibid.

4. Ibid.

5. Ibid.

INDEX

Symbols

A

B

C

cash-based business 21, 187, 189, 191, 193
Certified Divorce Financial Analyst™ (CDFA™) iii, 124, 301
child support 9, 12, 66, 98, 99, 102, 114, 117, 121, 179, 180, 182,
    185, 190, 193, 225, 227, 228, 229, 230, 231, 233, 234, 236,
    238, 239, 269
Chinitz, Marilyn B. 12, 13, 18, 38, 39, 226, 227
college tuition 111, 179, 182
commencement date 139
Community Property State 8, 54, 111, 134, 135, 157, 172, 175, 206,
    210
conflicting out 66
coping emotionally 81, 83, 85, 87
court 39, 41, 42, 52, 74, 76, 87, 98, 100, 101, 102, 103, 113, 115, 117,
    121, 125, 138, 159, 160, 166, 176, 182, 189, 200, 201, 205,
    207, 211, 217, 218, 220, 221, 229, 238, 242, 254, 268, 276, 296
custody 10, 25, 50, 51, 52, 66, 70, 87, 159, 160, 161, 162, 181, 220,
    269, 272, 276, 287
custody battle 25

D

Date of Separation 111, 129, 138, 139, 146, 156, 210
Davin, Kristin 83, 84, 85
debts 8, 11, 12, 111, 128, 133, 157, 175, 191, 200, 204, 296
dignity 283
DiMaggio, Debra 38, 39, 68, 71
disinheriting 29
dividing stock 133, 135, 137, 139, 143, 144
Divorce "Don'ts" 275
divorce financial advisor 19, 29, 61, 68, 82, 86, 116, 124, 125, 127,
    130, 147, 183, 192, 206, 217, 218, 231, 264, 271, 302
Divorce Financial Checklist 59, 69, 293
Divorce Financial Strategist™ 8, 226, 252
divorce team 5, 37, 60, 68, 70, 76, 86, 108, 109, 128, 153, 189, 193,
    198, 199, 206, 209, 217, 230, 231, 235, 272, 278, 285
dual citizenship 135, 137, 139, 143, 144, 267
dual nationality 268

E

email 73, 74, 277, 280

emergency fund 60

Employee Retirement Income Security Act (ERISA) 234, 235, 237, 238

Equitable Distribution State 54, 111, 134, 135, 157, 172, 173, 210, 211, 235

expenses 11, 23, 37, 38, 40, 44, 51, 59, 70, 113, 114, 116, 120, 121, 122, 123, 154, 173, 179, 180, 181, 182, 191, 198, 200, 201, 204, 205, 207, 262, 296, 297

F

Facebook 73, 74, 75, 227, 278, 279

federal tax law 15

filing first viii, 65, 66, 68, 69

Financial Affidavit viii, 26, 76, 113, 114, 116, 117, 120, 121, 122, 125, 205

forensic accountant 147, 193, 200

fraud 19, 190, 206

frequent flyer miles 165

G

gifts 2, 11, 62, 111, 115, 129, 139, 153, 156, 192, 199, 209, 210, 211, 212, 213, 214, 296, 297

H

hidden assets 8, 69

home 66, 68, 69, 297

I

income 37, 39, 43, 44, 59, 97, 99, 113, 114, 115, 116, 117, 120, 121, 122, 123, 136, 137, 148, 155, 174, 175, 188, 189, 190, 191, 192, 193, 196, 197, 198, 199, 200, 201, 204, 205, 207, 221, 225, 231, 239, 242, 246, 254, 255, 256, 261, 265, 293

indemnification 11, 12

inheritance 2, 25, 26, 111, 129, 156, 210, 211, 212, 213, 214, 263, 296, 297

Instagram 73
IRA 239, 295

J

joint accounts 37, 38, 40, 41, 42, 213, 214
joint tax returns 15, 19
Jolie, Angelina i, 40, 50, 66

K

Kaminski, Rami 82, 83, 85
Klum, Heidi i, 40, 50, 66

L

legal separation agreement 8, 9, 11, 12, 13, 19, 30
liability 11, 12, 295
life insurance 32, 33, 295
Lifestyle Analysis 111, 116, 117, 119, 120, 122, 123, 125, 191, 192, 206, 207
LinkedIn 73
litigate 185, 217, 219, 221
litigation 13, 42, 43, 138, 190, 219, 262
living expenses 11, 37, 116, 120, 122, 173, 191, 206, 297
long separation 8, 9, 10
Lundy, Matt 235, 236

M

marital assets 8, 11, 12, 13, 38, 40, 41, 48, 53, 62, 70, 123, 128, 129, 130, 131, 134, 135, 153, 154, 165, 166, 168, 172, 192, 196, 199, 211, 213, 263, 276
marital debt 2, 12, 171, 173, 174, 175
marital home 2, 47, 49, 51, 53, 139, 263
marital property 26, 48, 53, 54, 89, 111, 114, 128, 129, 134, 135, 139, 146, 153, 156, 157, 171, 172, 173, 174, 204, 210, 211, 212, 214, 245, 262
marital residence 50, 52, 53, 54, 154
Mason, Sr., Miles 146, 190, 197, 200
moral objection to divorce 17